The

Ruskin Bond has been writing for over sixty years, and now has over 120 titles in print—novels, collections of short stories, poetry, essays, anthologies and books for children. His first novel, *The Room on the Roof*, received the prestigious John Llewellyn Rhys Prize in 1957. He has also received the Padma Shri (1999), the Padma Bhushan (2014) and two awards from Sahitya Akademi—one for his short stories and another for his writings for children. In 2012, the Delhi government gave him its Lifetime Achievement Award.

Born in 1934, Ruskin Bond grew up in Jamnagar, Shimla, New Delhi and Dehradun. Apart from three years in the UK, he has spent all his life in India, and now lives in Mussoorie with his adopted family.

RUSKIN BOND
The Wise Parrot

RUPA

Published by
Rupa Publications India Pvt. Ltd 2017
7/16, Ansari Road, Daryaganj
New Delhi 110002

Sales centres:
Allahabad Bengaluru Chennai
Hyderabad Jaipur Kathmandu
Kolkata Mumbai

ISBN: 978-81-291-4648-9

First impression 2017

10 9 8 7 6 5 4 3 2 1

Printed at Thomson Press India Ltd., Faridabad

CONTENTS

CONTENTS

INTRODUCTION

'The Wise Parrot', 'Blue Beard', 'The Tiger-King…' ancient tales are full of colourful and fantastic creatures and characters. These days, not a day goes by that one doesn't hear about a new writer who is dazzling everyone with a new book. Some of them truly dazzle. Some others get forgotten and gather dust after a while. But the stories that live on, and have lived and grown with us over centuries, are the epics, legends, fairy tales and folktales from around the world.

I have always enjoyed gathering these stories from various places. European folklore and fairy tales would appear in books and magazines in my youth. Stories from the epics like the Mahabharata and the Buddhist legends in the Jataka tales I came across in books and through people I met in my youth. Once, while I was spending a few days with my friend Anil in his village in North India, I heard many stories of ghosts and fairies from his mother, who was a great raconteur. A few of those stories have appeared in my writings over the years. In the meanwhile, I kept up my hunt for ancient tales, and as more came my way, I stored and told and retold them to the great delight of my readers.

These tales can be twisted yet comical, wise while being simple. There are so many from India—there's 'Jivaka the Boy Wonder', whose tales have been heard in Indian, Tibetan and Arabian folklore; Heera and Lal whose friendship and stories of adventure are as fantastic as they are exciting; and the tale of the Tiger-King, whose promise of help would save a life when it was asked for. Stories from China and Japan are equally engrossing.

Scheherzade of the Arabian Nights told a thousand and one stories. I may be no Scheherzade, and that is a relief, for it would be rather difficult for me to think of stories knowing my head may be chopped off the next day, yet I have found some ancient legends that are as enthralling as hers and presented them here. There are tales of friendship and tales of betrayal. There are creatures who have lived in our collective imaginations for ages. There are stories of wit and stories of immense stupidity. And in all this, what shines forth is the power of the human imagination that has thrived for millions of years. From the first cave paintings, to today's novels, the thrill of telling a story has never died down. And here's wishing that may it live long, bringing people, animals, fairies and ghosts to life forever.

Ruskin Bond

JIVAKA THE BOY WONDER

A Tale from Ancient India

King Bimbisara, that mighty warrior whose fame has spread far and wide, had three sons, the youngest of whom was named Jivaka. The elder sons resembled their father. They had great muscular strength, were skilled in the use of arms, and displayed courage whether in battle against the fierce hill tribes or when hunting lions and tigers. Jivaka was a gentle youth, who took no pleasure in warlike sports, or in the society of warriors. He loved to walk about alone, and he rarely spoke unless he was spoken to.

The King was greatly troubled about Jivaka, and spoke to him, saying: 'Have you any ambition in life? You never join your brothers either when they engage in sports or when they go into the jungle to hunt wild beasts.'

Jivaka said: 'It is my desire, O honoured father, to become a learned man, and to earn my living as a physician.'

'It is not usual for kings' sons to become physicians.'

'But, O father, why should not the son of a king become a learned man?'

'I grant your wish,' the King said, 'but, as you do not require to earn your living, I cannot understand why you want to leave me. You are not able to take care of yourself like your elder brothers.'

Jivaka said: 'I shall disguise myself, and go into another kingdom where no man will know who I am.'

'I shall allow you to go,' said the King. 'The quest of wisdom is a noble one. Wherever you go, behave modestly. Honour those who know what you do not know. Learn from everyone, observe everything, and use your intelligence.'

Jivaka bade farewell to the King, his father, to the Queen, his mother, and to his brothers. He disguised himself, left the palace under the cover of night, and walked a great distance until he came to the house of a Brahmin. The Brahmin welcomed him, and said: 'Who are you, and what do you seek?'

Jivaka said: 'I desire to become a learned man.'

'Tarry with me for a time,' the Brahmin said, 'and be my disciple.'

Jivaka abode for a year in the Brahmin's house, and when he had learned everything the Brahmin could teach him, he asked leave to take his departure.

Before Jivaka went away the Brahmin said: 'Go to the hills and live a time among the fierce tribes that dwell there. They have great skill as trackers. Learn all they know, and you will benefit from their knowledge. Then go next to my brother, who is a great physician, and has skills in opening skulls to cure diseases of the head. When you have learned all he can teach you, go in search of the green jewel, which shines like a lamp, and will enable you to find out from what malady a sick man is suffering. I bless you and bid you farewell, O my son.'

Jivaka went away and did as the Brahmin advised him. He dwelt for a time among the fierce hillmen. They received him kindly because they saw that he was a young man of great modesty and kindly heart. In time they instructed him how to track wild beasts, and how to observe the tracks of every living creature on roadways, in the forests, and across wide plains. He spent three years among the hillmen, and he acquired great skills as a tracker.

After leaving the hillmen, who sorrowed to part with him, he dwelt with the Brahmin physician, and learned how to treat wounds and open skulls. He remained with this Brahmin for two years. The old physician became very fond of Jivaka because he was an excellent student, and soon became very skilful. When the young man bade him farewell, he said: 'You must now search for the green jewel, which is hidden in a young tree, the bark of which always sheds a fine dust. The wood of this tree is as heavy as iron.'

Jivaka turned his face southwards towards his father's kingdom, and travelled across wide plains and deep forests. One morning he reached the hut of an old Brahmin. This holy man had just recited his morning prayers, and was sitting on the side of the roadway in front of his dwelling.

Jivaka sat down beside him, and they spoke to one another for a while about holy things. Then the young man told the story of his travels, but he did not tell who he was.

The Brahmin said: 'I gather from what you say that you are a keen observer. Now, I shall put your skills to test. Can you tell me if any living creature went past me this morning?'

'I shall soon tell you,' the Jivaka said with a smile.

He walked along the road, and after a little time returned and sat down. Then he said: 'A man went past here this morning carrying wood. The burden was too heavy for him, because he was not only weak but also very thin.'

'You speak truly,' said the Brahmin.

'Afterwards an elephant went past. It was a female, and a woman led it. The elephant was crippled, having injured its left hind foot, and its right eye was blind.'

'You speak truly,' said the Brahmin.

'An hour went past, and then a man came driving a bullock-cart. He was in a hurry, and whipped the bullocks, and he had a dog which leapt about and barked at them.'

'If you had been sitting here beside me,' said the Brahmin, 'you could not have seen more.'

'Then,' said Jivaka, 'a thief crept out of the wood. He stood still for a few minutes when he caught sight of you, but as you were praying with closed eyes he ran past, and you did not observe him. As he has been wounded he cannot have gone far.'

'I know nothing of the thief,' said the Brahmin.

He had no sooner spoken than three soldiers rushed out of the woods and leapt on to the roadway. They looked first to the left and then to the right, but were unable to make up their minds which way they should go.

Jivaka watched them, and said: 'The thief entered the king's palace during the night, and these are three of the sentinels. They followed the thief, and saw him in the forest, where one wounded him with an arrow; but the fellow managed to hide himself, and lead them astray after he had bound his wound.'

Seeing the Brahmin and Jivaka sitting on the side of the road, the sentinels hastened towards them and spoke, saying: 'Have you seen a man passing this way?'

The Brahmin shook his head, but Jivaka said: 'He went past less than an hour ago. He is the thief you seek, and has been wounded by an arrow. How did it come about that you allowed him to escape in the woods?'

'Have you spoken to him?' asked one of the sentinels.

'No,' Jivaka answered, 'I have not even seen him.'

'Then how do you know that we are pursuing a thief, and that he has been wounded?'

'I shall explain to you afterwards. Hasten onwards to the left, and you shall find him not far from here.'

'You know more about the man than you will confess to,' said one of the sentinels. 'You had better, therefore, come with us.'

'As you will,' answered Jivaka. He rose up to go with the sentinels, and, turning to the Brahmin, said: 'Wait here until I return.'

Jivaka walked in front of the sentinels, gazing at the ground. They began to ply him with questions, but he said: 'Keep silent, lest the thief should hear you and take alarm. I shall answer all your questions when we find him.'

They went on together in silence after that. In time they reached the ruins of an old house. Jivaka placed his right hand over his mouth as a sign to the men not to speak. Then he pointed towards the house. The sentinels crept forward stealthily, and, entering the house, found the thief lying in a corner fast asleep. They seized and bound him, and carried him outside.

'Where is the jewel that you have stolen?' asked a sentinel.

The thief answered, saying: 'What jewel? I do not know what you mean. Why have you seized me and bound me?'

'You stole the magic jewel from the king's house.'

'Oh, no! You are mistaken. You have followed the wrong man.'

'It was you whom we pursued in the forest. You were wounded by an arrow in the thigh. I see you have bound the wound.'

'It was I whom you wounded,' the thief said, 'but I am innocent. I was sleeping in the forest when I heard you coming. Thinking you were robbers I fled away, and when you wounded me I hid myself because I dreaded that you desired to slay me for some reason or other.'

The man seemed to be speaking the truth, and one of the sentinels said: 'If this is not the thief, we shall be punished for our folly.'

Jivaka did not say a word. He knelt beside the man, who had been laid on a grassy bank, and examined his hands and feet. Then he undid the bandage on his thigh, and, having placed healing leaves on the wound, he bound it skilfully. The prisoner thanked him and blessed him, saying: 'My wound does not pain me now, O physician.'

'Do you know this man?' a sentinel asked, speaking to Jivaka.

Jivaka said: 'I have never set eyes upon him before, but I shall tell you what I know about him. He is a potter, and last night entered the palace garden and climbed an ashoka tree. He concealed himself among its branches until it was nigh to midnight. Then he crept down and entered the palace through the servants' quarters, knowing his way well, because he has often sold earthenware pots to the chief cook. In the darkness he made his way to the room in which the jewel is kept. The room is covered with deerskin rugs. When he found the jewel he left the palace through a window, and, grasping a trailing plant, slipped down to the ground, but when he was near the ground the plant snapped and he fell. For a time he lay stunned on the ground. Then, hearing cries of alarm being raised within the palace, he ran through the garden, climbed the wall, and hastened towards the forest.

'By this time the moon had come out from behind the clouds, and you caught sight of him and followed him. In the forest you shot many arrows, and one wounded him in the thigh. He concealed himself amidst the undergrowth, and when you had gone past him he rose up, having bound his wound, and made his way towards the highway. He saw a Brahmin praying in front of his hut and ran past him. As his bandage had become loose he readjusted it, but having lost much blood he found he was not able to go far. Seeing this ruined house, he made up his mind to hide in it, but before entering it he hid the jewel in a clay-hole.'

The thief gasped with wonder as Jivaka spoke. 'You are a magician,' he said.

Jivaka spoke sternly, saying: 'Now lead us to the spot in the clay-hole where you have hidden the jewel.'

The sentinels unbound the man and he rose. He led them to a clay-hole behind the ruined house, and, lifting a stone, took up a ball of wet clay, which he broke in two. The jewel dropped out, and Jivaka caught it and handed it to the chief sentinel.

The sentinels and the thief marvelled greatly to meet so wise a man as Jivaka, and they paid him great deference as they walked with him back to the place where they had left the Brahmin. The Brahmin greeted them and said: 'You have found the thief and the jewel also.'

The chief sentinel said: 'You speak truly; but we would not have been successful had not this wise young man gone with us. Pray tell me,' he said, addressing Jivaka, 'what is your name?'

Jivaka gave him a strange name, and said: 'Now that I have served you well, allow me to bid you farewell.'

The sentinels bowed and took their departure. Then Jivaka sat down beside the Brahmin.

Brahmin said: 'Now tell me all that took place.'

Jivaka told him. Then the Brahmin said: 'Now tell me how you knew that there passed along the roadway this morning a thin man carrying wood, a crippled elephant led by a woman, and a bullock-cart driven by a man who whipped the bullocks, and was accompanied by a dog which leapt about and barked at the slow animals?'

Jivaka answered, saying: 'It has always been my custom to make close observations. All that I told you I saw on the empty roadway. I saw the footprints of the man who carried wood. He walked heavily on his heels, and his footprints showed that his feet were thin. I knew, therefore, that he was a thin man. As he walked he swayed from side to side. I knew, therefore, that his burden was heavy; and I knew he carried wood because the dust of the bark is sprinkled along the highway in his tracks.'

'Tell me how you knew that the elephant came along after the man had passed.'

'Because, O master, some of the man's footprints had been trodden over by the elephant.'

'How did you know that the elephant was a female?'

'A male elephant leaves round footprints, and a female elephant leaves oblong footprints. The footprints of this elephant are oblong. Observe them for yourself.'

'How did you know that the elephant was crippled?'

'Because it pressed lightly with the left hind foot, which has been injured.'

'How did you know its right eye was blind?'

'The elephant cropped grass from the bank as it went along, but it cropped on the left side only, and when the woman led it to the other side of the road it did not crop at all.'

'How did you know that a woman led it?'

'A woman's footprints are different from those of a man.'

'Now tell me how you knew that the bullock-cart followed after the elephant?'

'The tracks of the cart crossed some of the footprints of the elephant.'

'And how did you know that the driver was in a hurry and that he whipped the bullocks?'

'Because the distances between the bullocks' hoof-marks were so unequal. When the driver whipped them, they sprang forward at a quickened pace; their tracks were then made deeper and they were closer together. I knew by the tracks of the dog that it leapt about and barked at the bullocks. Having pondered over the tracks, I saw, as in a vision, an angry and impatient driver who made the bullocks quicken their pace by whipping them, and also urged his dog to bark at them.'

'It seems all so simple,' said the Brahmin. 'Still, I cannot understand how you knew so much about the thief. How did you find out that he had hidden in a tree, and, entering the palace through the servants' quarters, made his way to a room covered with deerskin rugs? Tell me also how you came to know that he went through a window and slid down a creeper which broke, so that he fell to the ground and lay stunned there, and how you found out that he fled through the forest, passed this spot when my eyes were closed, ran onwards towards the clay hole, where he hid the jewel, and then concealed himself in the ruined house?'

Jivaka said: 'I shall tell you, O Brahmin, how I discovered the thief's secret. First of all I observed his footprints leading from the woods. He tiptoed across the tracks of the bullocks. Therefore I knew that he came after the bullock-cart had passed. Three times he paused because he saw you. Then he crossed the road and ran lightly. In the spots where he paused, his footprints were impressed fully and clearly. When he ran he left the marks of the forepart of his feet only. I knew, therefore, that he was a guilty man. He did not want you to see him, and I concluded you did not see him because your eyes were closed in prayer.'

'Wonderful!' exclaimed the Brahmin. 'Now tell me how you came to know about his doings last night after you had tracked him to the ruined house?'

Jivaka said: 'I examined very closely his hair, his body, his hands, and fingernails, his legs, his toes, and his toenails. I also examined his wound and the bandage that was wrapped round it.'

'And what did you see?'

'I knew he was a potter because the palm of his right hand was smooth, while the palm of his left hand was rough. Potters turn their wheels with their left hands, and the wheel hardens the skin. I saw seeds of the ashoka tree in his hair, and knowing that no ashoka tree is to be found near the king's palace except in the garden, and that the seeds would not have fallen in his hair unless he had pressed his head among the branches, I concluded he had climbed the tree after scaling the wall; he would not have dared to enter through the gate, which is guarded by sentinels; therefore, he must have climbed the wall. I saw red sand in his toenails. Red sand is strewn daily round the servants' quarters, and, as he is a potter, I concluded he had been in the habit of selling pots to the chief cook. By making regular visits to the palace, and hearing the conversation of the servants, he must have learned where the jewel was kept.'

'I follow your reasoning, O wise young man,' said the Brahmin.

Jivaka continued: 'The potter was greatly excited when he entered the palace. Men who are excited perspire freely. As I examined his body, I saw that there was hair from deerskins on it. There was also hair under the upper part of his toenails. He must have lain on the rugs for a time. Hair clung to his body-cloth and the bandage with which he had bound his wound.'

'But how did you know,' asked the Brahmin, 'that he left the room through a window?'

Jivaka said: 'There were green and purple stains on both his hands. These came from the crushed leaves and blossoms. Besides, two of his fingers on the left hand and one on the right were cut as if by a cord. He must have slipped down quickly to have his fingers cut so. Anyone who slides down so frail a thing as a creeper is sure to break it; so I examined his body carefully and saw bruises on his left hip, his left elbow and his left ear. I concluded therefore that he had fallen, and was made certain of this when I saw black earth in his hair on the left side of his head. He must have lain for some time on the ground, because the earth was caked on his hair. That was because the earth was damp with dew. He would not have lain there unless he had been stunned.'

'Your reasoning is wonderful. It delights my heart!' said the Brahmin.

Jivaka continued: 'I saw that there were scratches on his knees, and that they were inflicted after he had lain on the deerskin rugs, because some hairs had been pressed into them. I concluded he had climbed the wall hurriedly. I also noticed that three of his toenails on the right foot had been bent inward, and as there was red sand inside them I knew they had been bent after he had left the palace. Of course, it was to be expected that he would climb the wall, seeing there were sentinels at the gate, but he would not have climbed hurriedly unless he had been alarmed.'

'How did you know,' asked the Brahmin, 'that the moon rose after he had scaled the wall?'

'He would not have been seen otherwise. Men do not shoot arrows in the dark, and this man was wounded by an arrow.'

'No wonder the thief confessed his guilt,' the Brahmin said. 'He must have thought you were a magician. The only thing that puzzles me now is, how you knew the man had hidden the jewel in the clay-hole, because you never went near it.'

'Passing along the way a few days ago,' explained Jivaka, 'I saw the clay-hole behind the ruined house. There are other ruined houses on the other side of the clay-hole. Once upon a time, several potters lived with their wives and families in these houses, but finding the clay had become of inferior quality they deserted their little village and went elsewhere. This man, being a potter, was probably born in the house in which he hid himself, and being a potter he could think of no better place than a clayhole in which to hide something of value, for no man, except a potter, ever thinks of entering a dirty clay-hole.'

'I am glad you have come this way,' said the Brahmin. 'Tarry with me and let us converse together. It is many years since I met with a man of such great intelligence.'

Jivaka said: 'I must walk to the nearest inn, because I wish to purchase the wood that the thin man was carrying.'

'Why do you wish to purchase it?' asked the Brahmin.

'Come with me and you will know.'

The Brahmin walked with Jivaka towards the inn, and when they reached it they saw the thin man sitting in front of it. He was very poor, and was waiting for someone to offer him food.

Jivaka spoke to the man, saying: 'Will you sell the wood you have been carrying?'

'Yes, master,' answered the beggar.

'Name your price, then.'

The man named his price, and Jivaka paid it, although the Brahmin thought it far too high.

Jivaka carried the wood back to the Brahmin's hut, and examined each piece very carefully. Then he split one piece and took out a green jewel. 'At last, I have found it,' he said. 'I knew by the dust that fell from the bark that the thin man had found and cut down the tree I had been searching for.'

The Brahmin was greatly surprised. 'What jewel is this?' he asked.

Jivaka said: 'He who possesses it will become a great physician. When it is placed near a sick man it will shine like a lamp and reveal what malady he is suffering from.'

'I would like to see it tested,' said the Brahmin.

He had not long to wait, for soon afterwards a beggar came along the road wailing and beating his head.

'What ails you, poor man?' asked the Brahmin.

'Alas! O master, my head pains me as if someone were stabbing it with a dagger.'

Jivaka said: 'Allow me to examine your head.'

The beggar sat down, and Jivaka placed the green jewel on his head. Then he said: 'A centipede has crawled in through your ear, and is eating its way through to your brain.'

'Oh, cure me, master!' cried the beggar.

Jivaka made the man dig a hole and go into it. The earth was then heaped up to his neck, so that he could not move. When this was done, Jivaka opened his skull, and, seizing the centipede with pincers, took it out. Then he closed the skull, put healing herbs on the wound, and bandaged the man's head. When the beggar was taken out of the hole, and given food to eat, he said that his pain had gone. He thanked Jivaka, and went on his way.

'If the king hears of your skill,' said the Brahmin, 'he will appoint you his chief physician.'

He had hardly spoken the words when the soldiers who had arrested the thief came hastily towards his hut. The chief sentinel spoke to Jivaka, saying: 'His Majesty the King, having heard from me of your wonderful powers of observation, desires to see you and converse with you. Come with us now to the palace.'

'Very well,' Jivaka answered, 'I shall go.'

He bade farewell to the Brahmin, who was grieved to part with him, and went to the palace with the soldiers.

The King actually suffered from a tumour which grew out of his head, and his physicians were unable to deal with it. When Jivaka was brought before him, he said: 'Have you knowledge of the art of healing?'

Jivaka bowed, and said that he had. He spoke in a strange voice, because he perceived that the King, his father, did not recognize him.

First of all Jivaka prepared a ripening poultice, which caused the tumour to grow larger. Then he used the green jewel, and saw that he could deal with the tumour without further delay. He asked the King to go into his bath. When His Majesty did so, Jivaka poured many jugfuls of hot water, in which herbs had been soaked, over the tumour. Then he touched the tumour with his lancet, and poured more water over it, until the tumour emptied itself. The King felt no pain, and did not know that the lancet had been used.

Next, Jivaka applied healing herbs, which caused the wound to close quickly and become quite whole.

'Now feel your head,' Jivaka said.

The King passed his hand over his head, and was greatly astonished to find that the tumour had been taken away. He called for a mirror, but although he looked closely into it he was unable to find the exact spot where the tumour had been. After the King had partaken of a meal, he called his ministers together, and said: 'See, the young physician has cured me. I shall appoint him chief physician.'

Jivaka was called before the King, who spoke to him, saying: 'I appoint you my chief physician, O honourable young man. I shall also reward you because of the help you gave to my soldiers, when they were searching for the thief who stole my precious jewel. I pray you, tell me who you are and whence you come, and how you have become so learned a man, although still quite young.'

Jivaka said: 'O King, I have become a learned man because I have obeyed the command of my father. He told me to travel through the world alone in search of wisdom. He bade me observe everything and use my intelligence.'

'Who is your father?' asked the King.

Jivaka prostrated himself at His Majesty's feet, and said: 'Behold! O King, I am your son, Jivaka.'

The King was overcome with joy. He raised his son and embraced him, and said: 'This is indeed a happy day, for once more I hold in my arms the son of my heart, whom I have long yearned for.'

Jivaka was appointed the King's chief minister as well as his chief physician, and he lived happily ever afterwards, loved and admired by all.

THE GREEN MAN OF SINAI

A Tale from Ancient Egypt

The desert of Sinai is haunted by a little old man, who may often be seen wandering among the sand-hills and across the bare limestone ridges. He is usually met with in the grey twilight, when camels are tethered and tents are set up, and fires are lit to cook the evening meal. Nobody ever speaks to him, and he never speaks to anyone, but when he comes near a camp he may gaze wistfully at it as he passes by. If a child should ask, 'Who is that little old man?' an Arab will answer, 'It is only El Kedir, the Wanderer, a poor old man who will never do anyone harm.'

And if a child should then say: 'Why is he walking past the camp when night is coming on? Why does he not come and ask for food and a bed?' the Arab will answer: 'He never eats and he never sleeps. He is always searching for what he will never find, and he takes no rest by day or by night.'

'Is he a spirit?' a child may ask.

'No, he is not a spirit; he is only a very old man.'

When the evening meal is eaten, and before children are put to bed in the little Arab tents, the story of El Kedir is sure to be told to those who have seen the strange old man for the first time.

'Now, hear the story of the Wanderer,' an Arab will say when the children gather round him in the light of the camp fire. 'I heard it long ago from my father, as my father heard it from his father. El Kedir has been wandering about in the desert for hundreds of years. No one knows rightly how old he is. Once upon a time he was a merchant in Mecca. He was a dealer in precious stones, and became very rich. It worried him very much to think that some day he must die and leave all his riches behind him. He read old books which tell of magic charms, and of herbs that help to prolong life and cure diseases, and he came to know that somewhere in the world there is a fountain called the Well of Life. He spoke to the priests and magicians about this wonderful well, and they told him that anyone who drank of its water would never die.

El Kedir said: 'Where is this Well of Life? I would fain drink of the water, because I fear death.'

A wise old priest made answer, saying: 'The Well of Life is in a far distant land. To reach it one must cross wide deserts and climb high mountains, which are infested with wild beasts. Beyond the mountains is a river full of crocodiles, and beyond the river is a deep forest, and beyond the forest is a high cliff which no man can climb. In the face of the cliff there is a cave, and the cave leads to the country of the Well of Life. The passage through the cliff is very long and very dark. It is also dangerous, because serpents and other reptiles swarm among the rocks, waiting to devour any man who dares to seek for the Well of Life. The reptiles can see in the darkness, and they fear light, because light blinds them.'

El Kedir said: 'Can a man not carry a torch to guide himself through the dark passage?'

The wise old priest shook his head. 'The passage is very long. If a man walks very quickly he cannot get through it in less time than a day and a night. No torch will keep burning for that length of time. Besides, blasts of wind sweep through the passage now and again, and these will blow out a torch, and before one can relight it the reptiles will attack the man who has dared to enter their dwelling-place.'

El Kedir's heart was sad when he heard of the perils of the dark passage, and he returned home to think out a plan which would enable him to get a draught of water from the Well of Life.

Next day he spoke to several men, and offered them much money if they would set out in search of the well, but no one dared to do so.

A year went past, and then a stranger came to El Kedir's house. He spoke to the merchant, saying: 'I have a jewel to sell. Will you buy it from me?'

El Kedir said: 'No. I have more jewels than I know what to do with.'

'But this jewel,' the stranger said, 'is unlike any other jewel in the world.'

The merchant said: 'Show it to me.'

The stranger opened his right hand, in which lay a small bright stone.

El Kedir said: 'Your jewel is not worth very much. I have many precious stones which are more costly and more beautiful.'

The stranger closed his hand. 'Darken the window,' he said, and then you will know something about this wonderful jewel.'

El Kedir drew a thick curtain across the window, and the room was then as dark as if it were midnight.

'Now, show me the jewel again,' he said.

The stranger opened his hand and revealed the jewel, which shone so brightly that the room was lit up as if the sun were still shining through the window.

El Kedir cried out with surprise. 'I have never before seen so bright a gem,' he said. 'Where did you find it?'

'I cannot tell you,' answered the stranger, 'but I did not steal it. This bright stone is called Light in Darkness, and also Adam's jewel, because it was found by our first father, Adam, in the Garden of Eden. Will you buy it from me?'

El Kedir was thinking of the Well of Life, and said: 'Will this jewel shine in the darkest cave, and lead me through the passage to the land of the Well of Life?'

The stranger answered, saying: 'Yes. The jewel will light up the darkest of places, and its light will never go out. It will also protect the man who owns it against all perils. No wild beast will attack him and no reptile will sting him, and when he is in need the jewel will cause the jinn to serve him when he needs their help.'

El Kedir said: 'What price do you ask for this jewel?'

The stranger drew aside the dark window curtain, so that the sunshine might stream into the room. Then he sat down and laid the jewel on a little table. 'It is priceless,' he said. 'If a king asked me what I wanted for it, I would ask for his kingdom.'

'Alas!' El Kedir said, 'I am not as rich as a king.'

The stranger said: 'Although you have not a kingdom to offer me in exchange for the jewel, yet you have great wealth. I shall give you Light in Darkness on condition that you give me in return all that you now possess—your house, your land, your slaves, your jewels, your gold, your silver, your ivory ornaments and your ornaments of ebony.'

El Kedir heaved a deep sigh. 'If I give you all I possess,' he said, 'I shall be a beggar.'

The stranger said: 'Ali, no! You will not be a beggar. You will be the richest man in the world, because you will possess Adam's Jewel.'

El Kedir said: 'I will give you half of my possessions for this precious stone.'

The stranger rose to his feet as if to leave.

'You are not going away, surely,' the merchant said.

'If you will not agree to my terms, I must certainly go at once,' replied the other very firmly. 'Listen to me. I will give you this jewel now on condition that you walk out of the house and leave me as master and owner of it. Not only must you leave the house, you must leave Mecca, and set out on your journey to find the Well of Life. What is your answer? Will you go now, or must I go away?'

'Give me a night to think it over,' El Kedir pleaded.

'No,' said the stranger; 'I have not time to spare. You must say yeah or nay now. What is your answer?'

As he spoke he opened his hand and displayed the gleaming jewel.

'It is priceless,' said El Kedir.

The stranger nodded.

El Kedir seized the jewel, and said: 'I agree to the bargain. I shall set out on my journey now. But tell me in what direction I must go.'

'The jewel will lead you,' the stranger said. 'Now go away. I am master and owner of this house.' He frowned and stamped his foot.

El Kedir was startled. He realized all at once that he had parted with everything he possessed, and he fled from the house and made his way towards the western gate of the city. As he passed through the streets many people saluted him, but he took no notice of their salutations.

'Has El Kedir gone mad?' men asked one another. El Kedir himself wondered if he was in his right mind as he passed through the western gate and set out to cross the desert. He wandered on and on, not knowing whither he was going, until he became very weary. The afternoon went past, and still he trudged on his aimless way. Not until the sun began to set over the bleak desert hills did he pause to look around. He was hungry and thirsty, and he feared that he would faint and perish. 'Alas!' he cried, 'I have been a fool. I have given away all my possessions for this useless jewel.'

He sat down on the sand and began to examine the jewel. Tears sprang to his eyes. 'Alas!' he sighed. 'The stranger bewitched me, and now I must perish for my folly. Would I have food to eat and water to drink! Would I have a tent to sleep in and servants to attend to me!'

He had no sooner spoken than a man appeared beside him and laid a hand on his shoulder.

El Kedir looked up. 'Who are you?' he asked.

The man bowed. 'I am your servant,' said he. 'Come with me and I will give you all you ask for.'

El Kedir rose to his feet and followed the man, who walked round the shoulder of a bare hill and entered a cave. With wonder and joy El Kedir saw a table spread in the cave. It was loaded with dainties. 'I have been waiting for you,' the man said.

Servants brought water and washed El Kedir's feet and hands. Then they gave him wine to drink. Feeling refreshed, the weary merchant began to eat, and he ate until he was satisfied. Afterwards he lay down to rest on a soft couch, and soon he fell asleep.

In the morning, when El Kedir awoke, he gazed round about in surprise, for he found himself alone in the midst of the desert. The cave had vanished; even the hill had vanished. 'I have been dreaming,' he said. 'Would I had water to drink and food to eat!'

He rose up and looked around, and, to his surprise, saw on a flat stone a jar of water and a bunch of figs. He drank the water and ate of the fruit until he was satisfied. Then he realized that he could obtain anything he desired simply by wishing, because he possessed the wonderful jewel that grants all desires.

He held the jewel in his right hand and said: 'I want a camel to ride on and servants to attend upon me.'

In a minute a man came towards him, leading a camel. This man bowed to El Kedir and said: 'I am your servant. How many attendants do you wish to have with you on your journey?'

El Kedir said: 'As many as you think I require for protection against robbers and wild beasts.'

The man clapped his hands thrice, and three armed men mounted on camels came in sight.

'Whither would you go?' the man asked next. El Kedir said: 'It is my desire to visit the land in which I shall find the Well of Life.'

'I shall lead you thither,' the man said, 'but you must go through the dark underground passage alone.'

El Kedir said: 'Very well. So be it.'

The camel knelt on the sand and El Kedir mounted it. Then, following his guide, he set out on his journey towards the land of his desire.

For seven days El Kedir and his attendants travelled westward. Each evening they found a camp prepared for them, and in it plentiful supplies of water and food.

On the evening of the seventh day they reached a camp below a ridge of high mountains, and, when darkness came on, El Kedir heard lions roaring as they came forth to seek for their prey. He seized the jewel and said: 'May the lions cease to roar! May every wild beast leave this place until I go away!'

There was silence after that. El Kedir knew that his wish had been granted, and he lay down to sleep.

Next morning, as he sat in his tent eating figs, El Kedir spoke to his guide, saying: 'How shall we cross the mountains?'

'Call for the birds, and they will come hither,' said the guide. El Kedir seized the jewel and called for the birds.

No sooner had he done so than he heard a loud noise like the noise of a tempest. He looked up and saw great birds flying towards the camp. They had wings like the sails of an ocean ship, and bodies big as camels.

'We shall ride on their backs,' said the guide. 'They will carry us across the mountains.'

The birds alighted on the sand and crouched low to allow El Kedir and his servants to mount them. Although of great bulk, the birds were very beautiful. Their bodies were of bright gold, and their wings were coloured like the rainbow.

As soon as El Kedir and his attendants were mounted on their backs, the great birds rose high in the air and began their flight. El Kedir looked down and he saw, as if from the top of a high hill, the great desert he had crossed and the rocky steeps and great chasms he was being carried over. The wild beasts that prowled among the mountains looked up as the birds flew towards the west. Beyond the mountains there was a broad river, and El Kedir knew it was the River of Crocodiles. It ran through a green and fruitful valley, and beyond it there was a deep forest of mighty trees.

When the mountains were crossed the birds alighted on the left bank of the river, and El Kedir and his companions leapt down from their backs. Then they flew away.

El Kedir gazed at the river and saw many crocodiles. 'Would these reptiles move away!' he said. When he had spoken thus, hundreds of crocodiles took flight as if pursued by an enemy. Then El Kedir said, 'I have need of a boat.'

He had no sooner spoken than a ferryman appeared, rowing a boat from the opposite bank. As soon as he came near enough, El Kedir and his attendants stepped into the boat and sat down. The ferryman spoke not a word to them. He conveyed them over the river, and when they stepped ashore he returned to the middle of the river, where his boat sank and disappeared. El Kedir then knew that the ferryman was a spirit being.

After resting and partaking of food, El Kedir and his attendants walked towards the forest. It was pleasant to enter its shadowy depths for the sun was hot and there was not a cloud in the sky. The music of birds and the humming of insects made sweet music in their ears. Flowers of every hue adorned the beautiful forest, and the air was full of their sweet odours.

They walked on until they came to an open space in which there was a gleaming pool. Brightly coloured fish swam to and fro in the clear water. The sight of the pool filled El Kedir's heart with joy, and he said: 'Here could I dwell for the rest of my days and feel content.'

When he had spoken thus, his chief attendant bowed before him and said: 'Master, we can go no farther. Permit us to bid you farewell.'

El Kedir said: 'If you must go, then I must say "farewell", but fain would I reward you first.'

No sooner did he say 'farewell', however, than his attendants were changed into fishes. They leapt into the pool and were lost among the others that swam there. El Kedir then knew that his attendants were spirit beings. He began to feel afraid, and turned away from the pool. The sun was setting, and the sky was lit up by the golden rays of evening. Birds ceased to sing, insects vanished, and a silence deep as death fell on the forest. El Kedir turned towards the west and walked on. Twilight came on and darkness followed swiftly. Then the Wanderer feared he would be lost. 'Alas!' he cried, 'I fear to pass the night alone in the forest. Would I find a dwelling in which to lie down and rest in safety!'

He had no sooner spoken than he saw a light twinkling among the trees. Wondering greatly, he walked towards it, and soon found that it shone from the open door of a house. He entered the house, and saw a little old man sitting on the floor. On a low table beside him were baskets of ripe fruit and two stoups of wine.

El Kedir bowed to the little old man, and said: 'I am a traveller, and desire food and a bed.'

The old man greeted him pleasantly, saying: 'You are welcome. Come and sit with me. I am just about to partake of supper.'

As he spoke he clapped his hands, and two dark-skinned servants came out of the shadows. They bowed to El Kedir, and brought him water to wash himself. When he had washed, they clad him in raiment of green silk, and put a red turban on his head.

El Kedir felt happy and comfortable, and sat down to partake of supper. The little old man asked him whence he came and whither he was going, and he told him that he came from Mecca and was searching for the Well of Life.

The old man said: 'Have you got the jewel that the stranger gave you?'

El Kedir answered 'Yes', and showed the jewel in the palm of his right hand.

'It is well,' the old man said, 'On the morrow you will follow the path which leads from my house towards the cave. Holding the jewel in your hand, you will enter the dark passage, which swarms with venomous reptiles. Then you will throw the jewel before you, and walk towards the place where it falls. As soon as you reach it, you will pick it up and throw it before you again. Thus, throwing the jewel before you, I promise that you will go through the dark passage in safety. When you reach the Well of Life, you can drink of its water if you so desire, but before you drink, turn the jewel round three times, and bid the guardian of the well to appear before you. When you return through the dark passage, throwing the jewel before you, cone to this house and I will give you further instructions.'

Near morning El Kedir bade farewell to his host, and walked towards the cave. He peered into it, and as he did so he heard strange noises, like the rushing of winds, and the beating of wings, and the rustling made by reptiles as they creep to and fro. A cold shiver went through his body, and he feared to enter the cave. He sat down on the ground for a time, wondering whether he should go on or turn back. The wood was very silent, but soon the silence was broken by the sound of breaking twigs. He looked towards the place whence the sound came, and was horrified to behold a great black serpent creeping towards him. 'Alas!' he cried. 'Who art thou?'

The serpent reared its shaggy head, and answered him, saying: 'I am the messenger of Death.'

'Come not near me,' El Kedir said, taking the jewel from his pouch and grasping it firmly in his right hand.

The black snake coiled itself and answered him, saying: 'I cannot follow you, but I can prevent you from returning, O man of timid heart!'

El Kedir was greatly terrified, and ran into the cave. As he did so, he flung the jewel in front of him. When he did this, the cave was lit up, and the reptiles that lay in his path fled and hid themselves, for the bright rays of Adam's jewel had blinded them and made them afraid. El Kedir walked on, and when he reached the jewel he picked it up and flung it in front of him again. He then saw that the passage was long and narrow. Indeed, it was not wide enough for more than one at a time to walk through it. El Kedir went on and on, flinging the jewel before him. Now and again blasts of wind blew through the passage, and made him stumble as he pressed forward, and when the wind fell a deep and dreadful silence followed, and in the silence he heard the noise of the creeping reptiles far behind him and far in front of him. On and on he went, fearing to rest and feeling faint and hungry, and at length he said: 'Would I have water to drink and fruit to eat!'

He had no sooner spoken than he heard the noise of falling water. The sound was pleasant to his ears, and when he reached the jewel he found that it had fallen in front of an inner cave in which there was a waterfall and a deep pool. He stooped down and drank of the water, and then bathed his hands and his feet and washed his face. Feeling refreshed, he rose up and gazed round the cave. In a small recess he saw a silver table piled up with ripe fruit and rich golden-coloured cakes. He went towards it and ate till he was satisfied. Then, feeling strong and active again, he picked up the jewel and went on his way, flinging it in front of him along the dark passage.

On and on he went, until at length he reached the end of the passage, which led into a beautiful garden. El Kedir gazed at the garden with eyes of wonder. Never before had he seen such bright flowers and such stately trees. He marvelled greatly, but he marvelled still more when he found that the blossoms and flowers on the trees were jewels of priceless value, and that the trunks and branches of the trees were of silver and gold.

In the midst of the garden was a green pool, which twinkled in the rays of the sun.

El Kedir feasted his eyes on the beauties of the garden. Then, after a time, he remembered what the little old man had told him. Accordingly he turned the jewel round three times and said: 'May the guardian of the Well of Life appear before me!'

When the words were spoke, a beautiful woman, clad in garments that shone like silver, appeared before him. 'Alas!' she said. 'Why have you come hither?'

El Kedir said: 'It is my desire to find the Well of Life.'

The woman pointed towards the green pool in the middle

of the garden, and said: 'That is the Well of Life.'

El Kedir uttered a cry of joy; but the fair lady said to him: 'Beware of the pool! If you drink of the water you will never again enjoy the companionship of mankind. You will become a stranger without a home and without a friend.'

El Kedir said: 'If I drink of the water I will cease to fear death.'

'Yes, you will cease to fear death,' the lady answered with a sigh, 'but you will begin to dread life.'

El Kedir laughed. 'I have come a long journey. I have gone through many perils,' he said, 'and now that I have found the Well of Life, you ask me not to drink. I have given away all I possess for the jewel named Light in Darkness, so that I might come hither, and yet you ask me not to drink of the magic water. If I turn back now without drinking the water, the black serpent will attack me and I will die; and if I escape the serpent and return to Mecca, all men will mock me and spurn me because I have parted with my possessions for a useless jewel. No, no; I will not take your advice. I must drink of the water of the Well of Life.'

The lady guardian of the well made no answer, but faded from his sight in a ray of dazzling sunshine.

El Kedir was weary, and went towards the shining pool. Stooping down, he lifted water in the palm of his right hand and sipped it. When he did so his weariness left him and he felt refreshed. The water was cool and sweet and inviting, and casting off his garments El Kedir plunged into it. He bathed his whole body and drank many great draughts of the water. It seemed to him then that he had become young again. His limbs were full of vigour and strength, and when he left the pool lie began to dance with joy.

As he danced, the ripples passed off the surface of the pool and it became quite clear again. El Kedir looked into the water and then he discovered that all his body had turned green. He gazed upon his arms and legs with astonishment, and exclaimed: 'Alas! What has happened to me? I am now a green man.' That is how he came to be called El Kedir, which means 'the Green One'.

A sadness fell upon his heart, and he wondered what the people of Mecca would say when they beheld him again.

'I shall return home without delay,' he said to himself.

He entered the dark passage again, throwing the jewel in front of him as he went, and when lie had passed through, and returned to the forest, he hastened towards the house of the little old man.

The old man was sitting at the door of his house waiting for him.

'You have tasted the water of the Well of Life,' the old man said.

'Yes,' El Kedir answered, 'but my skin has turned green.'

'You have paid the penalty,' said the old man. 'I advise you not to return again to Mecca, but to dwell here.'

El Kedir said: 'I came hither to drink the magic water so that I might be able to enjoy life. I must, therefore, return to Mecca.'

'You will not be welcomed by your fellows.'

'You jest.'

'Besides, you cannot return again without my help.'

'What do you mean?'

'The birds that flew over the mountains will not carry you back to the desert unless you give me Adam's jewel.'

'Alas!' El Kedir said, 'The jewel is all I possess. I gave the stranger all my possessions for it.'

'But you have had your reward. You have drunk of the water of the Well of Life.'

'Must I then return to Mecca as poor as a beggar?'

'Yes, my friend. That is why I have advised you to remain here.'

El Kedir was silent for a time. Then he said: 'No, I cannot stay with you. I long for my old friends. I would rather return to Mecca as a beggar than remain here forever. I have become young again; I can set to work and make another fortune and enjoy life. Take the jewel and help me to return home.'

'As you will,' said the little old man, who took the jewel from El Kedir and placed it in his breast. 'Now, lie down and sleep.'

El Kedir said: 'Will you not offer me fruit to eat and water to drink?'

'You have no need of food or water,' the old man said, 'because you have drunk the magic water.'

El Kedir laughed and said, 'Will I never need to eat and drink again?'

'No, never,' the little old man said.

El Kedir said: 'Then I shall soon become a rich man again.'

He lay down to sleep. When he awoke he found himself lying on the desert sand, because while he had slept he had been carried back by spirit beings to his native land. He stood up and gazed about him.

The desert was wrapped in darkness, and out of the darkness a voice spoke to him, saying: 'You have slept your last sleep. You will never sleep again, and yet you will not feel weary.'

El Kedir clapped his hands with joy. 'I shall no longer have to eat, or drink, or sleep,' said he. 'How fortunate I am! I shall soon become very rich, and all men will envy me.'

He saw lights twinkling in the darkness and walked towards them. Soon he reached the wall of a large town. Sentinels stood at the gate, and he spoke to them, saying 'What city is this?'

A sentinel said: 'This is the city of Mecca. Who are you, and whence come you?'

El Kedir gave his name, and asked permission to enter through the gate.

The sentinel, who had already spoken, said: 'The gate will be opened at dawn. Then you may enter.'

El Kedir sat down, waiting for the dawn. When the first ray of light appeared in the east the gate was opened, and he rose to enter the city. The sentinels allowed him to go past, but no sooner had he passed them than they uttered cries of horror and fled away to the right and to the left.

El Kedir wondered why the sentinels had behaved in this strange manner, but did not wait to ask. He walked on until he reached the marketplace. There he saw a woman carrying a jar of water on her head. He spoke to her, saying: 'You have gone early to the well.'

The woman turned round and looked at him. As soon as she did so she uttered a cry of dismay, dropped the jar, which was shattered on the roadway, and fled from him.

The sun rose and the air grew bright. El Kedir walked through the marketplace and saw several slaves coming towards him carrying bales of silk. He waited till they came near, but as soon as their eyes fell upon him they flung down their bales and ran away, crying: 'The green man! The green man!'

Then El Kedir's heart was filled with dismay. 'Alas!' he said, 'I am feared by everyone. I must hide myself.'

He left the marketplace, and, seeing an empty house, crept into it through a broken window. There he remained until the people passed up and down the streets in increasing numbers. He peered out through a slit in the door of the old house, and at length saw many merchants whom he knew and with whom he had done business. He longed to speak to them, and at length he ventured to leave the house. To conceal his face he drew his robe across it, and he blackened his hands and legs with soot. Thus disguised, he left the house and entered the marketplace. Many eyes followed him as he passed along. 'Who is that man?' one asked another. 'Why does he hide his face?'

El Kedir walked towards a group of dealers in precious stones, and sat down in front of them.

'Who comes hither?' asked one, gazing with wonder on the form of El Kedir.

'You will know my voice,' El Kedir said.

'It is the jewel merchant who gave all he possessed to a stranger,' said one of the dealers.

'Yes, indeed, it is I and no other,' El Kedir answered. The men laughed because he had said: 'It is I.'

'Why do you hide your face?' one asked.

Before El Kedir could answer, a woman who stood near him shrieked, and cried out with horror: 'He casts no shadow. He is an evil spirit.'

The dealers sprang to their feet, and one of them seized El Kedir's garment and rent it in twain. Then everyone saw that his face was green, and his body and his limbs were also green.

Men, women, and children fled at once from the marketplace, crying: 'The green man! The green man!'

Then El Kedir realized that he could never live among his fellow men again, because everyone feared him. He returned to the empty house and hid himself until darkness fell. Then he came out and fled through the streets towards the western gate.

The gate was already closed, but he asked the sentinels to open it. At first they refused to do so, one of them saying: 'Who are you that dares to command us to open the gate?'

'I am the Green Man,' El Kedir answered. 'Let me go forth, and I shall never again return.'

The sentinels opened the gate and he ran out of the city. The gate was closed quickly behind him.

In this manner El Kedir left his native city to wander alone in the desert. It is said that he is still wandering about searching for the spirit guide who led him westward towards the land of the Well of Life, and that when night falls he hears voices calling him through the darkness. He has been wandering up and down the desert for long years—indeed, for hundreds of years. He cannot rest, he never sleeps, and he cannot die, because he has drunk of the water of the Well of Life.'

When an old Arab tells this story to the young people the children pity the desert wanderer. 'Poor old man,' a woman may say, 'perhaps he will be forgiven in time, and allowed to lie down and die.'

THE STORY OF THE BIRD FENG

A Fairy Tale from China

In the Book of the Ten Thousand Wonders there are three hundred and thirty-three stories about the bird called Feng, and this is one of them.

Ta-Khai, Prince of Tartary, dreamt one night that he saw in a place where he had never been before an enchantingly beautiful young maiden who could only be a princess. He fell desperately in love with her, but before he could either move or speak, she had vanished. When he awoke he called for his ink and brushes, and in the most accomplished willow-leaf style, he drew her image on a piece of precious silk, and in one corner he wrote these lines:

> The flowers of the peony
> Will they ever bloom?
> A day without her
> Is like a hundred years.

He then summoned his ministers, and, showing them the portrait, asked if any one could tell him the name of the beautiful maiden; but they all shook their heads and stroked their beards. They knew not who she was.

So displeased was the prince that he sent them away in disgrace to the most remote provinces of his kingdom. All the courtiers, the generals, the officers, and every man and woman, high and low, who lived in the palace came in turn to look at the picture. But they all had to confess their ignorance. Ta-Khai then called upon the magicians of the kingdom to find out by their art the name of the princess of his dreams, but their answers were so widely different that the prince, suspecting their ability, condemned them all to have their noses cut off. The portrait was shown in the outer court of the palace from sunrise till sunset, and exalted travellers came in every day, gazed upon the beautiful face, and came out again. None could tell who she was.

Meanwhile, the days were weighing heavily upon the shoulders of Ta-Khai, and his sufferings cannot be described; he ate no more, he drank no more, and ended up forgetting when was day and when was night, what was in and what was out, what was left and what was right. He spent his time roaming over the mountains and through the woods crying aloud to the gods to end his life and his sorrow.

It was thus, one day, that he came to the edge of a precipice. The valley below was strewn with rocks, and the thought came to his mind that he had been led to this place to put an end to his misery. He was about to throw himself into the depths below when suddenly the bird Feng flew across the valley and appeared before him, saying:

'Why is Ta-Khai, the mighty Prince of Tartary, standing in this place of desolation with a shadow on his brow?'

Ta-Khai replied: 'The pine tree finds its nourishment where it stands, the tiger can run after the deer in the forests, the eagle can fly over the mountains and the plains, but how can I find the one for whom my heart is thirsting?'

And he told the bird his story.

The Feng, which in reality was a Feng-Hwang, that is, a female Feng, rejoined: 'Without the help of Supreme Heaven it is not easy to acquire wisdom, but it is a sign of the benevolence of the spiritual beings that I should have come between you and destruction. I can make myself large enough to carry the largest town upon my back, or small enough to pass through the smallest keyhole, and I know all the princesses in all the palaces of the earth. I have taught them the six intonations of my voice, and I am their friend. Therefore, show me the picture, O Ta-Khai, and I will tell you the name of her whom you saw in your dream.'

They went to the palace, and, when the portrait was shown, the bird became as large as an elephant, and exclaimed, 'Sit on my back, O Ta-Khai, and I will carry you to the place of your dream. There you will find her of the transparent face with the drooping eyelids under the crown of dark hair such as you have depicted, for these are the features of Sai-Jen, the daughter of the King of China, and alone can be likened to the full moon rising under a black cloud.'

At nightfall they were flying over the palace of the king just above a magnificent garden. And in the garden sat Sai Jen, flute singing and playing upon the flute. The Feng-Hwang deposited the prince outside the wall near a place where bamboos were growing and showed him how to cut twelve bamboos between the knots to make the flute which is called Pai-Siao and has a sound sweeter than the evening breeze on the forest stream.

And as he blew gently across the pipes, they echoed the sound of the princess's voice so harmoniously that she cried: 'I hear the distant notes of the song that comes from my own lips, and I can see nothing but the flowers and the trees; it is the melody the heart alone can sing that has suffered sorrow on sorrow, and to which alone the heart can listen that is full of longing.'

At that moment the wonderful bird, like a fire of many colours come down from heaven, alighted before the princess, dropping at her feet the portrait. She opened her eyes in utter astonishment at the sight of her own image. And when she had read the lines inscribed in the corner, she asked, trembling: 'Tell me, O Feng-Hwang, who is he, so near, but whom I cannot see, that knows the sound of my voice and has never heard me, and can remember my face and has never seen me?'

Then the bird spoke and told her the story of Ta-Khai's dream, adding: 'I come from him with this message; I brought him here on my wings. For many days he has longed for this hour, let him now behold the image of his dream and heal the wound in his heart.'

Swift and overpowering is the rush of the waves on the pebbles of the shore, and like a little pebble felt Sai-Jen when Ta-Khai stood before her.

The Feng-Hwang illuminated the garden sumptuously, and a breath of love was stirring the flowers under the stars.

It was in the palace of the King of China that were celebrated in the most ancient and magnificent style the nuptials of Sai Jen and Ta-Khai, Prince of Tartary.

And this is one of the three hundred and thirty-three stories about the bird Feng as it is told in the Book of the Ten Thousand Wonders.

THE FRIENDSHIP OF HEERA AND LAL

In a certain town there lived a poor grass-cutter who made his living by cutting grass in the forest and selling it in the town for a few paisa. One day, as usual, he rose early in the morning and went into the forest. When he had cut sufficient grass, he found that he had left behind the rope with which he usually tied the bundle. He was very upset, because this meant he had lost a day's labour and earnings; but, as he was walking home despondently, he saw what appeared to be a glistening rope lying a few paces ahead of him.

The grass-cutter took the rope in his hand, and, as he did so, it changed into a long, green snake. He dropped the snake; and, as the reptile touched the ground, it resolved itself into a ruby, or lal, of great value.

The grass-cutter had no idea of the value of what he had found; but, tying it in his turban, he returned home. Next morning he went to the palace and presented his find to the Raja.

The Raja was so pleased with the ruby that, certain that his Rani would admire so beautiful a stone, he took it into her apartment and presented it to her. But as soon as the Rani took the stone in the palm of her hand she found that it was no longer a ruby but a beautiful new-born baby.

As the Rani had no children of her own, she adopted the child, and brought him up with care and affection. When Lal was eight years old, he was sent to a school where only the children of royal families were taught. There he met an enchanting Princess called Heera, and they became close friends.

As the years passed, and the boy and girl grew older in each other's company, their young love grew stronger. When the Raja, Lal's foster-father, heard of their friendship, he immediately ordered the boy to stop seeing Heera. Meanwhile, Heera's parents, for political reasons, announced the engagement of their beautiful daughter to a powerful Raja who was old, one-eyed and bent double. When Lal heard of the betrothal, he ran out of his father's palace, mounted a swift horse, and rode to the kingdom of Heera's father.

He reached the city on the day of the marriage. The bride came out of the palace followed by a long procession, and people marched with lights and drums through the gaily decorated streets. As the procession passed down the main street, Heera caught sight of Lal. And while the celebrations were at their height, she slipped away and joined him. Then, disguising herself as a boy—so that she resembled Lal very closely—she rode out of the city with him.

They rode fast and far, the hooves of their steeds giving out sparks of fire as they thundered through the forests. On and on they rode until the sun went down and the stars came out. And after several days they reached a large city, where they took lodgings at an inn.

When they were passing through the streets the next day, they noticed a woman sitting near a cooking-pot, weeping bitterly.

'Why are you weeping, mother?' asked Heera.

'Don't you know, my child?' said the woman. 'The Raja of this city has a beautiful daughter for whom every day a young man is sacrificed. Now it is the turn of my son, and these are the last sweets I shall ever make for him.'

'Do not weep, mother,' said Heera, 'We will go instead of your son to this terrible princess.' And they rode to the palace where the Raja's officers showed them into the chamber of the princess.

At first the princess treated him with great kindness; but later, when she was alone with Lal, a sudden change came over her. She began foaming at the mouth and tearing her hair. She rolled on the ground, and writhed and screamed. Heera rushed into the room. At the same time the exhausted princess fell into a deep coma, and, as she lay unconscious, her left thigh burst open, and a terrible black snake emerged from it.

The snake darted towards Heera with a great hiss, its forked tongue darting in and out. But Lal drew his sword and cut off the snake's head with a single blow.

They remained all night with the unconscious princess, and by morning she had come to her senses.

When the Raja came to know that the snake which had possessed his daughter for so long had been killed by two brave youths, he called them before him, and offered them whatever they liked.

'Announce our betrothal to each other,' requested Heera. 'Permit us to be married in your city.'

'But you are a boy,' said the Raja.

'No, I am the Princess Heera in the guise of a boy. And this is my consort, Prince Lal.'

The Raja immediately made them welcome as his guests, and his daughter and Heera became close friends. But as the day of the marriage drew near, the princess began to grow jealous. She was afraid that Lal would take Heera away from her.

One day the princess asked Heera: 'Tell me, dear sister, what is the caste of our dear friend Lal? Though we know he is the adopted son of a Raja, there is some mystery about his birth. I have heard it said that his real father was a mere grass-cutter.'

'Does it matter?' asked Heera. 'Am I not happy in his love, and in his delightful presence? What need is there to know his caste?'

But the princess persisted with her questioning, and made Heera promise that she would ask Lal about his caste.

One evening as Heera and Lal sat beside each other on the banks of a small river, she put her question to him.

Lal looked very distressed, and said, 'Heera, do not expect me to answer that question. Is it important to you?'

But Heera's curiosity was now aroused. She was bent on knowing the truth, and kept questioning Lal.

The boy walked a little way into the river, and said, 'Are you determined to know my caste?'

'Yes,' said Heera. 'You must tell me.'

He walked deeper into the river until the water reached his shoulders, and again he asked, 'Do you still want to know my caste, Heera?'

And Heera, thinking it was all a game, answered playfully, 'Yes, I do!'

Then Lal moved deeper into the water, until his body was submerged and only a tuft of his hair could be seen on the surface. And his voice came from under the water, asking, 'Heera, are you still bent upon knowing my caste? There is time to change your mind!' His voice sounded deep and strong, as though he was already speaking from another world.

But Heera did not waver in her resolution, and answered, 'I do. I do!'

As soon as she had spoken, the tuft of hair disappeared. In the place where Lal had been standing, there appeared a beautiful white lily, and on it lay a sparkling ruby. The flower and the ruby were visible for only a few moments. Then they vanished.

Heera waited day and night for Lal to reappear; but she waited in vain. He never came back.

THE WISE PARROT

Once upon a time there was a Raja who owned a parrot, and its name was Hiramantota.

This parrot was so very wise that the Raja would always consult it before attending his Court. Hiramantota was also very good at predicting the weather and days of good fortune, and the Raja and his ministers, whenever they wanted to go out hunting or on a long journey, would consult the wise parrot before choosing a day on which to start out.

One afternoon, when Hiramantota was sitting in the Court, a flock of parrots flew past the open door and settled noisily in some guava trees that grew in the gardens.

The Raja was most surprised when Hiramantota turned to him and said, 'Those are my people, perched on the guava trees. They have come to ask me to visit the country where I was born and bred. Please give me permission to take a holiday, so that I may visit my old home and see my parents and relatives again.'

But the Raja was disturbed by the parrot's request.

'If you go away, Hiramantota,' he said, 'who will advise me and help me to make correct decisions? And how do I know that you will return from that distant country where your people live?'

Hiramantota felt hurt that the Raja should doubt his loyalty.

'You know, O Raja, that I never break my word,' he said. 'If I promise that I will return upon a certain day, you know that

I will do so. Moreover, upon my return, I will bring you a truly wonderful fruit which has the rare quality of giving immortality to those who eat it.'

The Raja's curiosity was aroused by the parrot's description of this unusual fruit, and, although he was reluctant to part with Hiramantota even for a short time, he agreed to let him go for a week.

Hiramantota flew off with a shrill scream of delight, and joined the flock of parrots in the guava trees. For a few minutes there was a great chattering in the trees, and then, at a given signal, they all rose into the air and flew off in a westerly direction in the track of the setting sun.

Hiramantota's father was king of all the birds in his native country, and he and his queen were delighted to see their son again. There was great feasting and rejoicing in honour of the visit. Time passed all too quickly, and at the end of the week Hiramantota told his parents, 'I must now return to my Raja. He is expecting me back tomorrow, and I must not disappoint him.'

'Go my son,' said the King of the birds, 'and if your master can spare you again, come and visit us next year.'

'I will try to come,' said, Hiramantota. And I have one favour to ask you. Will you allow me to carry back to my master a specimen of the fruit of immortality which grows in these forests?'

'Most certainly,' said the King, and he gave his son one of these wonderful fruits.

Some hours later, while the Raja and his Prime Minister were together in the council chamber, the parrot flew in at the open window and settled at the Raja's feet. In his beak he carried the golden fruit.

'A thousand welcomes, my Hiramantota!' cried the Raja, stooping down and caressing his friend. 'And is this the fruit of immortality of which you spoke?'

'It is,' said the parrot, laying the fruit on the King's throne. 'Those who partake of it shall never die.'

All eyes in the council chamber turned enviously upon the golden fruit.

The Raja considered for a moment, and then said, 'This precious fruit must not be wasted. Let us plant it in the ground, and raise from it a tree which will bear more fruits upon its branches. In that way, many people will benefit from it.'

The head gardener was sent for, and he was told to plant the fruit with great care in the royal gardens. When the young tree appeared, it was to be well watered, fenced around, and tended with great care.

And in time a plant did spring up from the fruit, and began to grow into a vigorous young tree. The Raja and the parrot both watched its growth with considerable pleasure and satisfaction.

The tree grew rapidly for it was well nourished and cared for. Fruits began to form upon it. And then a strange thing happened. On a certain night, one of the fruits fell on the ground and was poisoned by a snake which ran its tongue over it. In the morning, the head gardener, not knowing what had happened, chanced to pass by, and seeing one of the precious fruits lying on the ground, picked it up, put it into a basket, and took it straight to the Raja.

The Raja summoned Hiramantota and the Prime Minister, and said, 'Behold, here is the first fruit of our tree of immortality!' 'Do not eat it, Your Highness,' said the Prime Minister. 'The first fruit should be dedicated to the gods.'

The Raja was pleased with this advice, and sent soldiers to inform the priests that he would attend the principal temple on the morrow.

The Raja divided the fruit amongst the priests, assigning two pieces to each god. These portions, of course, the priests took for their own use; and no sooner had they eaten one of them than they fell into a profound sleep, from which they never awoke.

The Raja was thunderstruck and immediately consulted his Prime Minister.

'Their deaths must have been caused by the fruit of immortality,' said the Prime Minister. 'It appears to me that Hiramantota has done us a great evil by introducing this poisonous fruit into our country. It seems that he intended to kill you and your family in this way!'

The Raja was inclined to believe his Prime Minister, and summoning Hiramantota, he asked the parrot, 'For whom did you bring back this fruit of immortality?'

'For you, O King,' answered Hiramantota without any hesitation.

Then the Raja said bitterly, 'I have protected you all these years, and placed you in position of honour and trust, and you have repaid me by black ingratitude and most sinister plots against my life and the lives of my family and people.'

And without giving Hiramantota time to say a word in his own defence, he struck the poor bird a heavy blow with a stick, and killed him on the spot.

Then the Raja gave instructions to the head gardener to place a thorny fence around the tree, and ordered that no one was to visit the spot.

Now there happened to be a dhobi—a washerman—connected with the palace, whose married son lived with him. Unfortunately the dhobi's wife and the son's wife could not agree, and were frequently quarrelling with each other. This brought much grief to the dhobi and his wife. So much so that one day they decided that they could stand it no longer, and would put an end to their lives. Whilst discussing the matter, it occurred to the dhobi that some of the poisoned fruit from the Raja's tree would serve their purpose, so at night he stole into the gardens, pushed aside the thorny fence, and taking one of the fruits, returned home. Then he and his wife both ate of the fruit, and lay down—as they thought—to die.

But the result was very different from what they expected, for no sooner had they devoured the fruit than they suddenly shuffled off many weary years and became quite young again!

The dhobi sprang to his feet, exclaiming: 'Isn't this wonderful? I feel almost like a boy again!' And his wife gave a skip and a jump, and screamed: 'I'm a girl, I'm a girl! I can dance and sing again!'

It did not take long for the strange news to spread through the bazaars, and soon all the gossips were talking of the dhobi and his wife who had eaten of the fruit in the Raja's garden, and become quite youthful again. (Needless to say, they no longer wished to die.) In time the news reached the palace, and the Raja was amazed and very troubled when he heard the story. He instantly made enquiries of the gardener, and then learnt for the first time that the fruit the priests had eaten was not plucked from the tree, but picked off the ground.

'That unlucky fruit must have been poisoned by a snake!' cried the Raja in distress. 'And I sacrificed my faithful Hiramantota due to my own suspicious thoughts and lack of faith. My poor parrot, my best friend! I will rather see you again and beg your forgiveness than live for a thousand years!' The heart-broken Raja was never seen to smile again. The first lesson he taught his children was that the rulers of states should not lightly order a subject's execution, lest it prove an act of injustice, and bring lifelong sorrow in its wake.

SEVEN BRIDES FOR SEVEN PRINCES

Long, long ago there was a king who had seven sons—all of them brave, handsome and clever. The old king loved them equally, and the princes dressed alike and received the same allowances.

When they grew up they were given separate palaces, but the palaces were built and furnished alike, and if you had seen one palace you had seen the others. When the princes were old enough to marry, the King sent his ambassadors all over the country to search for seven brides of equal beauty and talent. The King's messengers travelled everywhere, saw many princesses, but could not find seven suitable brides. They returned to the king and reported their failure.

The King now became so despondent and gloomy that his chief minister decided that something had to be done to solve this problem. 'Do not be so downcast, Your Majesty,' he said. 'Surely it is impossible to find seven brides as accomplished as your seven sons. Let us trust to chance, and then perhaps we shall find the right brides.'

The minister had thought of a scheme and the princes agreeing to it, were taken to the highest tower of the fort, which overlooked the entire city as well as the surrounding countryside. Seven bows and seven arrows were placed before the princes, and they were told to shoot in any direction they liked. Each prince had agreed to marry the girl upon whose house the arrow fell—be she daughter of prince or peasant.

The princes took up the bows and shot their arrows in different directions, and all the arrows except that of the youngest prince fell on the houses of well-known and highly respected families. But the arrow shot by the youngest went beyond the city and out of sight.

Servants ran in all the directions looking for the arrow, and after a long search found it embedded in the branch of a great banyan tree, on which was sitting a monkey.

The King and his courtiers and the ministers held a hurried conference and decided that the youngest Prince should be given another chance with his arrow. But the Pince, to everyone's surprise, refused a second chance.

'No,' he said, 'my brothers have found good and beautiful wives, and that is their good fortune. But do not ask me to break the pledge I took before shooting the arrow. I know I cannot marry this monkey, but nor will I marry anyone else. I shall take the monkey home and look after her as a pet.'

And the youngest Prince went out of the city and brought the monkey home.

The six lucky princes were married with great pomp, the city celebrated with lights and fireworks, and there was music and dancing in the streets. People decorated their houses with mango and banana leaves. There was rejoicing all over the city, except in the house of the youngest Prince who, though alone and rather sad, had placed a diamond collar around the neck of his monkey and seated her on a chair cushioned with velvet.

'Poor monkey,' said the Prince 'you are as lonely as I, on this day of rejoicing. But I shall make your stay here a happy one! Are you hungry?' And he placed a bowl of delicious mangoes before her and persuaded her to eat them. He began to talk to the monkey and spent much time with her. Some called him foolish, or stubborn; others thought he was a little mad.

The King discussed the situation with his ministers and sons, determined to find some way of bringing the Prince to his sense and marrying him into a suitable family. But the young Prince refused to listen to the advice and entreaties of his father, brothers and friends.

Months passed, and the Prince had not changed his mind. Instead, he appeared to grow more attached to his monkey, and was often seen walking with her in the gardens of the palace.

At last the King called a meeting of all seven princes, and said, 'My sons, I have seen you all settled happily in life. Even you, my youngest, appear to be happy with your strange companion. The happiness of a father consists in the happiness of his sons and daughters. Therefore, I wish to visit my daughters-in-law and give them presents.'

The eldest son immediately invited his father to dine at his house, and the other sons repeated the invitation. The King accepted them all, including that of the youngest Prince. The receptions were very grand, and the King presented his daughters-in-law with precious jewels and costly dresses. Eventually it was the turn of the youngest son to entertain the King.

The youngest Prince was very troubled. How could he invite his father to a house in which he lived with a monkey? He knew his monkey was more gentle and affectionate than some of the greatest ladies in the land, and he was determined not to hide her away as though she was something to be ashamed of.

Walking with her in the garden, he said, 'What shall I do now, my friend? I wish you had a tongue to comfort me. All my brothers have shown their houses and their wives to my father. They will ridicule me when I present you to him!'

The monkey had always been a silent and sympathetic listener when the Prince spoke to her, but now he saw that she was gesturing to him with her hands. And, bending over her, he noticed that she was holding a piece of broken pottery in one hand. The Prince took the broken shard from her. Written on it in a beautiful feminine hand were these words: 'Do not worry, Prince. Go to the place where you found me, throw this shard of pottery into the hollow trunk of the banyan tree, and wait for a reply.'

The Prince hesitated at first, but decided that his problems could get no worse if he followed his monkey's advice. So, taking the broken bit of pottery, he went out of the city to the banyan tree.

It was a very ancient tree, hundreds of years old, with its branches and roots spreading out in a wide circle, and its leaves forming many curious little bowers. The trunk, though hollow within, was very wide and thick. Going up to it, the Prince threw the piece of pottery into the hollow, and stood back to see if anything would happen.

He did not have to wait long.

A very beautiful girl, dressed in green, stepped out of the hollow, and asked the Prince to follow her.

She told him that the queen of the fairies wished to see him in person.

The Prince climbed the tree, entered the hollow, and after groping about in the dark, was suddenly let into a dazzling and wonderful garden, at the end of which stood an imposing palace. An army of tall sunflowers bordered the garden. Between the flowers flowed a sweetly-scented stream, and on the bed of the stream, instead of pebbles, there were rubies and diamonds and sapphires. Even the light which lit up this new world was warmer and less harsh than the light of the Prince's world. He was led past a fountain of silver water, up steps of gold, and in through the mother-of-pearl doors of the palace. But the splendour of the room into which he was taken seemed to fade before the incomparable beauty of the fairy princess who stood before him.

'Yes Prince, I know your message,' she said. 'Do not be anxious, but go home and prepare to receive your father, the King, and your royal guests tomorrow evening. My servants will see to everything.'

Next morning, when the Prince awoke in his palace, an amazing sight met his eyes. The palace grounds teemed with new life. His gardens were full of fruit trees—mango, papaya, pomegranate and peach. Under the shade of the trees there were stalls where fruit, sweets, scents and sherbets were available. Children were playing on the lawns, and men and women were listening to music.

The Prince was bewildered at what he saw, and was even more amazed when he entered his palace and found it full of noise and activity. Tables groaned under the weight of delicious foods. Great chandeliers hung from the ceilings, and flowers filled the palace with their perfume.

At this moment a servant came running to announce that the King and his courtiers were arriving. The Prince hurried out to meet them. He took them into the reception hall, which was now beautifully decorated. Here dinner was served. Then everyone insisted on seeing the partner the Prince had chosen; they thought the monkey would be excellent entertainment after such a magnificent dinner.

The Prince could not refuse their request, and went gloomily through his rooms in search of the monkey. He feared the ridicule that would follow. This, he knew, was the King's way of trying to cure him of his stubbornness in refusing to break his pledge.

The Prince opened the door of his room and was nearly blinded by a blaze of light. There, on a throne in the middle of the room, sat the princess whom he had met in the banyan tree.

'Yes, Prince,' said the Princess. 'I have sent away the monkey and have come to offer you my hand.'

On hearing that his pet had gone, the Prince burst into tears. 'What have you done?' he said. 'Your beauty will not compensate me for the loss of my friend.'

Then the Princess, with a smile, said, 'If my beauty does not move you, let gratitude help you take my hand. See what pains I have taken in preparing this feast for your father and brothers. Be mine, sweet Prince, and you shall have all the riches and the pleasures of the world at your command.'

The Prince was indignant. 'I never asked these things of you, nor do I know what plot is afoot to deprive me of my monkey! Restore her to me, and I will be your slave.'

Then the Princess left her throne, and taking the Prince by the hand, spoke to him with great love and respect. 'You see in me your friend and companion. I took the form of a monkey to test your faith and sincerity. See, my monkey's skin lies in the corner.'

The Prince looked, and there in the corner of the room he saw the skin of the monkey.

Both he and the Princess seated themselves on the throne, and when she said, 'Arise, arise, arise,' the throne rose in the air and floated into the hall where the guests had gathered. The Prince presented his Princess to his father, and you can imagine the astonishment of the King and the guests who had come expecting to see a monkey as their hostess. The King gave any number of presents to his new daughter-in-law, and the whole land was soon praising the Prince and his beautiful Princess.

But who am I to describe the happiness of such wonderful people?

The other princes soon became envious of their youngest brother's good fortune, and began to plan his downfall.

'Brother,' they said to him one day, 'your wife is a Pari,

belonging to a race of people who are famous for their fickle and mischievous ways. We know that you still keep the skin which the Princess wore before. Why do you keep it with you? You never know when she might change her mind and become a monkey again! We suggest that you destroy the skin as soon as possible.'

The Prince thought over their suggestion, and seeing that they had a point, found the skin and threw it into a blazing fire. Immediately there were loud cries from the fire, and the Princess herself emerged from the smoke and rushed from the palace. And then the entire palace, the gardens, and everything the Pari had brought with her, vanished at the same time.

The Prince was heartbroken.

'But how can love exist between a man and a daughter of the air?' asked the King. 'She came from the air, and she has vanished into it. Do not weep for her.'

The Prince, however, was not to be consoled, and early one morning he slipped out of the city and went to the old banyan tree, hoping to find some trace of the Princess there; but the tree, too, had disappeared. For days and nights he wandered about the countryside, eating wild fruits and drinking from forest pools and sleeping under the stars, and everyday he went further and further away from his city. One day he came upon a man who was standing on one leg (holding the other foot in his hand) and crying, 'Once did I see you, appear once more!'

The Prince asked him what was wrong, and the man standing on one leg replied, 'I was hunting in these forests when I saw a very beautiful lady passing this way. She was running and would not stop, though I called to her. I was so struck by her beauty and her sadness that I was unable to move from this place.' And he repeated, 'Once did I see you, appear once more!'

'I am looking for her, too,' said the Prince.

'Then find her soon. And when you do, please let me see her once more. Take this stick of mine as a token. You may find it useful on the way, and it has the virtue of obeying the commands of its owner.'

The Prince now travelled for days through burning deserts, often calling the name of the Pari Princess, but getting no response. After bearing many hardships, he found an oasis where he quenched his thirst at a little stream. While he was resting in the shade of a tree, he heard the strains of a guitar, and going in search of the source of this music, he found a handsome youth of twenty bent over his instrument, absorbed in what he was playing. So sweet was the music that even the birds had fallen silent. The young man finished playing, heaved a deep sigh, and said.

'Once did I see you, appear once more!'

He, too, had seen the Pari rushing away, and had been so struck by her beauty that he had been unable to leave the spot where he had been playing his guitar. The musician gave the Prince his guitar, and told him that it was capable of charming every living thing within hearing. In exchange, he only wanted to see the Peri again when the Prince found her.

The Prince carried on with his journey, crossing mighty mountains and glaciers. One day, while he was trudging through heavy snow, he again heard a voice crying, 'Once did I see you, appear once more!'

This time it was a pale and haggard young man, who told the same story of having seen the Pari rushing over the mountains. And here he was, unable to leave the mountain peak until he saw the beautiful Princess again.

'Take this cap,' he told the Prince. 'It can make you invisible when you put it on, and might be useful in your search for the Peri. But when you find her let me see her again, or I shall surely perish here!'

Carrying the stick, the guitar and the cap, the Prince went over the mountains and into a valley where he found a temple of snow—the pillars, the roof, the spires, all made of snow. Within the temple the Prince found a yogi, naked except for a loin-cloth, sitting on air some three feet above the floor without any visible means of support. His whole body glowed in the light that filtered through the inner screen of the temple.

The yogi, opening his eyes and looking straight at the Prince, said, 'I know your story. The Princess you are looking for is the daughter of the king of the Paris, whose palace is on the top of Mount Caucasus. The lady is very ill, so take this pot of balsam, which has healing powers, and these wooden slippers which will transport you wherever you like.'

As soon as the Prince put on the wooden slippers, he rose high in the air and was carried at great speed over the mountains to the land of the Paris. He alighted outside a great city where, putting on the cap which made him invisible, he passed unchallenged through the gates.

Once in the city's main square, the Prince began playing his guitar and so sweet was the music that all the Paris thronged into the square to hear him play. The king, hearing that a wonderful magician was charming his subjects, came out to meet him. He was so bewitched by the music that he fell on his knees before the Prince and said, 'My daughter has been lying ill with a strange fever for many months. Cure her, I beg of you, for she is the light of my eyes and the hope of my old age.'

The Prince accompanied the King into the palace, on a golden chair carried by the Paris. He was taken to the Princess's apartments, and there he found his Pari Princess, sound asleep. He took the balsam the yogi had given him, and told the waiting women to apply it to their mistress's body. As soon as this was done the Princess sat up in bed, feeling much better. Recognizing the Prince, she was about to call him by his name when he put his finger to his lips and with his eyes begged her to be silent.

When the King found that his daughter had been cured, he said, 'Great saint, ask any boon from me.'

'Your daughter's hand in marriage, great king,' replied the Prince without any hesitation.

The King was enraged at the Prince's audacity and ordered his soldiers to seize the mendicant and throw him into prison. But the Prince put on his cap and became invisible, and ordered his stick to keep off the soldiers. The King, finding that the Prince had vanished except for the stick which was employed on the backs of the soldiers, begged for mercy.

'Forgive us!' he called. 'Show yourself again, and I promise that you will have whatever you desire.'

The Prince made himself visible again. 'I am sorry I had to use my powers against you,' he said. 'Now give me one of the flying chairs which only the Peris know how to make, and let it take both me and your daughter to my father's kingdom.'

The King of the Peris at once brought out his daughter, attended by three beautiful Paris. They joined the Prince in a handsome palanquin, which rose into the air and carried them back to the Prince's country.

He did not forget those who had helped him on his outward journey. The Prince took his three friends back with him to his kingdom, where they married the three Peris who had attended on the Princess. And they all lived happily ever after.

As for the Prince's brothers, when the King, their father, came to know of the mischief they had caused, he was so enraged that he disinherited them all and would have thrown them into prison had not the youngest Prince persuaded the King to pardon them. And so they were forgiven, and suitable pensions were settled on them.

THE MAORI FAIRY FISHERMEN
A Tale from New Zealand

There are fairies in New Zealand, and the Maoris call them Patu-Paiarehe. They have fair hair and white skins, and live among the hills, where they have secret dwellings. All day long they hide from human beings, but when darkness falls they come out in search for food. They often hold meetings in lonely places, at which they feast, and afterwards dance and sing merrily. These fairies are very clever, and the Maoris used to learn many things from them.

Like fairies elsewhere, they are said to steal babies and leave little fairy children, called changelings, in their places. The Maoris believe that the white-haired albinos among them are changelings, and that the fairies are so fond of them that they teach them some of their arts. It is said that the Maoris learned the art of making fishing-nets from their fairies. The Maori who made the first fishing-net was an albino named Kahoo-Koora. He lived a long time ago, and the story told about him is as follows:

One day when Kahoo-Koora was walking along a lonely part of the beach, at some distance from his native village, he saw large numbers of heads and tails of mackerel lying in heaps on the sand. He wondered who had caught so many fish, and looked about for the footprints of the fishermen, so that he might know to what tribe they belonged; but, much to his surprise, he could not see a single one. Then he knew that the fishers were fairies. He examined the heads and tails of the mackerel, and came to know that the fairies had been fishing during the night. He said to himself: 'They could not have caught all these fish with hooks. They must have used nets. If we knew how to make nets, we should be able to catch as many fish as the fairies.' Kahoo-Koora walked slowly towards his home, thinking over what he had seen; and, after a time, he made up his mind to watch the fairies catching fish, and, if possible, to obtain their net, so that he might find out how it was made. He told his wife about the matter, and she said: 'It is a dangerous thing to spy upon the fairies. They might kill you if they discovered you.'

Kahoo-Koora said: 'I shall be very careful. There is no moon tonight, and the fairies will not be able to see that I am a human being.'

When the sun had set, Kahoo-Koora set out to visit the part of the beach where the fairies were accustomed to catch mackerel. He reached the place just as the fairies arrived from the hills, and he had no time to hide himself. They ran up and down the beach calling out to one another, and when one of them spoke to Kahoo-Koora, saying: 'Why are you not helping?' he realized that he was being regarded as one of them. He did not, therefore, feel afraid.

A shoal of mackerel came close to the shore, and the fairies got busy at once. A canoe went out to drop the net into the water round the shoal, and then those who stood on the shore began to haul it in. As the fairy fishers worked the net, they kept singing:

The net here, the net there,
Haul the net and do your share;

> Drop the net into the sea,
> Haul the net right merrily.

When the net was hauled ashore, large quantities of mackerel were thrown on the beach. Kahoo-Koora did his share of the work. The fairies never dreamed that he was a human being, because Kahoo-Koora was an albino, and all fairies have white skin and fair hair.

The dawn was near at hand, and the fairies had to work very hard to gather up their catch, because they had to return to their dwellings, among the mountains, as soon as the sun rose above the horizon.

Kahoo-Koora noticed that the fairies did not divide the fish into equal lots, as do human fishers. Each one collected as many fish as he could, and, having gutted them, strung them together.

As they collected the catch, each one taking as many mackerel as he could carry away, the fairies kept singing:

> String the fish and haste away,
> All of you, ere break of day.

Now Kahoo-Koora was in no hurry to leave the beach before sunrise. It was his desire to delay the fairies, so that he might lay hands on their net. He made a slip-knot on the string, and each time he lifted up his share of the mackerel, the knot slipped, and the fish fell in a heap on the sand. Then he began to collect them again. Time and again the fairies left their own work to help him to string the fish. They knotted the string securely for their human companion, but each time Kahoo-Koora unfastened the knot, so that the fish might slip off as he lifted them up. He thus delayed the departure of the fairies, who grew very excited as they sang:

String the fish and haste away,
All of you, ere break of day.

Kahoo-Koora wanted to get the fairy net for himself, and that
was why he kept playing tricks with the fish. He was just putting
off time, so that the fairies would not be able to leave the shore
before daybreak. So well did he act his part, that at length the
sun began to rise, when two fairies began for the twentieth time
to string his fish for him.

In the growing light the fairies then saw that Kahoo-Koora
was not one of themselves, but a human being of the fairy race.
They cried out with alarm, because they could not punish him
in the daylight, for the sun blinded their eyes and made them
feel afraid. They called one to another:

Haste you! Haste as fast as you can!
He's not a fairy, but a man.

Throwing away their fish, and leaving their boat and net on the
shore, all the fairies ran towards the hills to hide themselves.
The sun rose brightly, and Kahoo-Koora was left alone on the
beach. He looked around, and, being well pleased with himself
for having tricked the clever fairies, he laughed long and loudly.

Then he examined the fairy boat, and found that it had been
made of flax. It was so light that he could lift it with one hand
and carry it under his arm. Then he picked up the net and spread
it out on a smooth bank of sand. It had been made of rushes,
and was so frail that he knew it could not be used again. He did
not care whether it could be used or not, however. All he wanted
to know was how it had been made. He sat down and studied it
closely, and when he had done so he took a long piece of cord
and began to make a net for himself. In this way he learned the
art of net-making, using the fairy net as a pattern.

Kahoo-Koora was well pleased with himself, and, rolling up the fairy net and the net he had made himself, he went home and hid both nets in his house. Then he told some of his friends that a large quantity of newly-caught fish was lying on the beach, where the fairies were wont to throw their catches. They went with him to the spot, and divided the fish between them.

Kahoo-Koora afterwards made two or three large nets, and taught the fishermen how to use them. The Maoris could then catch fish in big quantities like the fairies.

Kahoo-Koora never needed to catch fish for himself. He was kept busy making nets, and men came from distant villages to buy them. He was asked for so many nets that he had to teach his children how to make them.

For the rest of his life Kahoo-Koora was called the 'Net-maker'. When he grew old he gave the airy net to his eldest son, who kept it as a pattern. Kahoo-Koora's descendants were famous net-makers for many generations, and the story of how the first net was made was handed down from father to son. Times have changed in New Zealand, but the Maori mothers still tell their children many stories about the white fairies who dwell among the hills, and of the wonderful things they used to do in the great old days.

THE TIGER-KING'S GIFT

Long ago in the days of the ancient Pandya kings of South India, a father and his two sons lived in a village near Madura. The father was an astrologer, but he had never become famous, and so was very poor. The elder son was called Chellan; the younger Gangan. When the time came for the father to put off his earthly body, he gave his few fields to Chellan, and a palm leaf with some words scratched on it to Gangan. These were the words that Gangan read:

From birth, poverty;
For ten years, captivity;
On the seashore, death.
For a little while happiness shall follow.

'This must be my fortune,' said Gangan to himself, 'and it doesn't seem to be much of a fortune. I must have done something terrible in a former birth. But I will go as a pilgrim to Papanasam and do penance. If I can expiate my sin, I may have better luck.'

His only possession was a water jar of hammered copper, which had belonged to his grandfather. He coiled a rope round the jar, in case he needed to draw water from a well. Then he put a little rice into a bundle, said farewell to his brother, and set out. As he journeyed he had to pass through a great forest. Soon he had eaten all his food and drunk all the water in his jar. In the heat of the day he became very thirsty.

At last he came to an old, disused well. As he looked down into it he could see that a winding stairway had once gone round it down to the water's edge, and that there had been four landing places at different heights down this stairway; so that those who wanted to fetch water might descend the stairway to the level of the water and fill their water-pots with ease, regardless of whether the well was full, or three-quarters full, or half full or only one quarter full.

Now the well was nearly empty. The stairway had fallen away. Gangan could not go down to fill his water-jar so he uncoiled his rope, tied his jar to it and slowly let it down. To his amazement, as it was going down past the first landing place, a huge striped paw shot out and caught it, and a growling voice called out: 'Oh Lord of Charity, have mercy! The stair is fallen. I die unless you save me! Fear me not. Though King of Tigers, I will not harm you.'

Gangan was terrified at hearing a tiger speak; but his kindness overcame his fear, and with a great effort, he pulled the beast up.

The Tiger-King—for it was indeed the Lord of All Tigers bowed his head before Gangan, and reverently paced round him thrice from right to left as worshippers do round a shrine.

'Three days ago,' said the Tiger-King, 'a goldsmith passed by, and I followed him. In terror he jumped down this well and fell on the fourth landing place below. He is there still. When I leaped after him I fell on the first landing place. On the third landing is a rat who jumped in when a great snake chased him. And on the second landing, above the rat, is the snake who followed him. They will all clamour for you to draw them up.

'Free the snake, by all means. He will be grateful and will not harm you. Free the rat, if you will. But do not free the goldsmith, for he cannot be trusted. Should you free him, you will surely repent of your kindness. He will do you an injury for his own profit. But remember that I will help you whenever you need me.'

Then the Tiger-King bounded away into the forest.

Gangan had forgotten his thirst while he stood before the Tiger-King. Now he felt it more than before, and again let down his water-jar.

As it passed the second landing place on the ruined staircase, a huge snake darted out and twisted itself round the rope. 'Oh, Incarnation of Mercy, save me!' it hissed. 'Unless you help me, I must die here, for I cannot climb the sides of the well. Help me, and I will always serve you!'

Gangan's heart was again touched, and he drew up the snake. It glided round him as if he were a holy being. 'I am the Serpent-King,' it said. 'I was chasing a rat. It jumped into the well and fell on the third landing below. I followed, but fell on the second landing. Then the goldsmith leaped in and fell on the fourth landing place, while the tiger fell on the top landing. You saved the Tiger-King. You have saved me. You may save the rat, if you wish. But do not free the goldsmith. He is not to be trusted. He will harm you if you help him. But I will not forget you, and will come to your aid if you call upon me.'

Then the King of Snakes disappeared into the long grass of the forest.

Gangan let down his jar once more, eager to quench his thirst. But as the jar passed the third landing, the rat leaped into it.

'After the Tiger-King, what is a rat?' said Gangan to himself, and pulled the jar up.

Like the tiger and the snake, the rat did reverence, and offered his services if ever they were needed. And like the tiger and the snake, he warned Gangan against the goldsmith. Then the Rat-King—for he was none other—ran off into a hole among the roots of a banyan tree.

By this time Gangan's thirst was becoming unbearable. He

almost flung the water-jar down the well. But again the rope was seized, and Gangan heard the goldsmith beg piteously to be hauled up.

'Unless I pull him out of the well, I shall never get any water,' groaned Gangan. 'And after all, why not help the unfortunate man?' So with a great struggle—for he was a very fat goldsmith—Gangan got him out of the well and on to the grass beside him.

The goldsmith had much to say. But before listening to him, Gangan let his jar down into the well a fifth time. And then he drank till he was satisfied.

'Friend and deliverer!' cried the goldsmith. 'Don't believe what those beasts have said about me! I live in the holy city of Tenkasi, only a day's journey north of Papanasam. Come and visit me whenever you are there. I will show you that I am not an ungrateful man.' And he took leave of Gangan and went his way.

'From birth, poverty.'

Gangan resumed his pilgrimage, begging his way to Papanasam. There he stayed many weeks, performing all the ceremonies which pilgrims should perform, bathing at the waterfall, and watching the Brahmin priests feeding the fishes in the sacred stream. He visited other shrines, going as far as Cape Comorin, the southernmost tip of India, where he bathed in the sea. Then he came back through the jungles of Travancore.

He had started on his pilgrimage with his copper water-jar and nothing more. After months of wanderings, it was still the only thing he owned. The first prophecy on the palm leaf had already come true: 'From birth, poverty.'

During his wanderings Gangan had never once thought of the Tiger-King and the others, but as he walked wearily along in his rags, he saw a ruined well by the roadside, and it reminded him of his wonderful adventure. And just to see if the Tiger-

King was genuine, he called out: 'Oh King of Tigers, let me see you!' No sooner had he spoken than the Tiger-King leaped out of the bushes, carrying in his mouth a glittering golden helmet, embedded with precious stones.

It was the helmet of King Pandya, the monarch of the land.

The king had been waylaid and killed by robbers, for the sake of the jewelled helmet; but they in turn had fallen prey to the tiger, who had walked away with the helmet.

Gangan of course knew nothing about all this, and when the Tiger-King laid the helmet at his feet, he stood stupefied at its splendour and his own good luck.

After the Tiger-King had left him, Gangan thought of the goldsmith. 'He will take the jewels out of the helmet, and I will sell some of them. Others I will take home.' So he wrapped the helmet in a rag and made his way to Tenkasi.

In the Tenkasi bazaar he soon found the goldsmith's shop. When they had talked awhile, Gangan uncovered the golden helmet. The goldsmith—who knew its worth far better than Gangan—gloated over it, and at once agreed to take out the jewels and sell a few so that Gangan might have some money to spend.

'Now let me examine this helmet at leisure,' said the goldsmith. 'You go to the shrines, worship, and come back. I will then tell you what your treasure is worth.'

Gangan went off to worship at the famous shrines of Tenkasi. And as soon as he had gone, the goldsmith went off to the local magistrate.

'Did not the herald of King Pandya's son come here only yesterday and announce that he would give half his kingdom to anyone who discovered his father's murderer?' he asked. 'Well, I have found the killer. He has brought the king's jewelled helmet to me this very day.'

The magistrate called his guards, and they all hurried to the goldsmith's shop and reached it just as Gangan returned from his tour of the temples.

'Here is the helmet!' exclaimed the goldsmith to the magistrate. 'And here is the villain who murdered the king to get it!'

The guards seized poor Gangan and.marched him off to Madura, the capital of the Pandya kingdom, and brought him before the murdered king's son. When Gangan tried to explain about the Tiger-King, the goldsmith called him a liar, and the new king had him thrown into the death-cell, a deep, well-like pit, dug into the ground in a courtyard of the palace. The only entrance to it was a hole in the pavement of the courtyard. Here Gangan was left to die of hunger and thirst.

At first Gangan lay helpless where he had fallen. Then, looking around him, he found himself on a heap of bones, the bones of those who before him had died in the dungeon; and he was watched by an army of rats who were waiting to gnaw his dead body. He remembered how the Tiger-King had warned him against the goldsmith, and had promised help if ever it was needed.

'I need help now,' groaned Gangan, and shouted for the Tiger-King, the Snake-King, and the Rat-King.

For some time nothing happened. Then all the rats in the dungeon suddenly left him and began burrowing in a corner between some of the stones in the wall. Presently Gangan saw that the hole was quite large, and that many other rats were coming and going, working at the same tunnel. And then the Rat-King himself came through the little passage, and he was followed by the Snake-King, while a great roar from outside told Gangan that the Tiger-King was there.

'We cannot get you out of this place,' said the Snake-King. "The walls are too strong. But the armies of the Rat-King will bring rice-cakes from the palace kitchens, and sweets from the shops in the bazaars, and rags soaked in water. They will not let you die. And from this day on the tigers and the snakes will slay tenfold, and the rats will destroy grain and cloth as never before. Before long the people will begin to complain. Then, when you hear anyone passing in front of your cell, shout: 'These disasters are the results of your ruler's injustice! But I can save you from them!' At first they will pay no attention. But after some time they will take you out, and at your word we will stop the sacking and the slaughter. And then they will honour you.'

'For ten years, captivity.'

For ten years the tigers killed. The serpents struck. The rats destroyed. And at last the people wailed, 'The gods are plaguing us.'

All the while Gangan cried out to those who came near his cell, declaring that he could save them; they thought he was a madman. So ten years passed, and the second prophecy on the palm leaf was fulfilled.

At last the Snake-King made his way into the palace and bit the king's only daughter. She was dead in a few minutes.

The king called for all the snake-charmers and offered half his kingdom to any one of them who would restore his daughter to life. None of them was able to do so. Then the king's servants remembered the cries of Gangan and remarked that there was a madman in the dungeons who kept insisting that he could bring an end to all their troubles. The king at once ordered the dungeon to be opened. Ladders were let down. Men descended and found Gangan, looking more like a ghost than a man. His hair had grown so long that none could see his face. The king did not remember him, but Gangan soon reminded the king of how he had condemned him without enquiry, on the word of the goldsmith.

The king grovelled in the dust before Gangan, begged forgiveness, and entreated him to restore the dead princess to life.

'Bring me the body of the princess,' said Gangan.

Then he called on the Tiger-King and the Snake-King to come and give life to the princess. As soon as they entered the royal chamber, the princess was restored to life.

Glad as they were to see the princess alive, the king and his courtiers were filled with fear at the sight of the Tiger-King and the Snake-King. But the tiger and the snake hurt no one; and at a second prayer from Gangan, they brought life to all those they had slain.

And when Gangan made a third petition, the Tiger, the Snake and the Rat-Kings ordered their subjects to stop pillaging the Pandya kingdom, so long as the king did no further injustice.

'Let us find that treacherous goldsmith and put him in the dungeon,' said the Tiger-King.

But Gangan wanted no vengeance. That very day he set out for his village to see his brother, Chellan, once more. But when he left the Pandya king's capital, he took the wrong road. After much wandering, he found himself on the sea-shore.

Now it happened that his brother was also making a journey in those parts, and it was their fate that they should meet by the sea. When Gangan saw his brother, his gladness was so sudden and so great that he fell down dead.

And so the third prophecy was fulfilled:

'On the sea-shore, death.'

Chellan, as he came along the shore road, had seen a half-ruined shrine of Pillaiyar, the elephant-headed God of Good Luck. Chellan was a very devout servant of Pillaiyar, and the day being a festival day, he felt it was his duty to worship the god. But it was also his duty to perform the funeral rites for his brother.

The sea-shore was lonely. There was no one to help him. It would take hours to collect fuel and driftwood enough for a funeral pyre. For a while Chellan did not know what to do, but at last he took up the body and carried it to Pillaiyar's temple.

Then he addressed the God. 'This is my brother's body,' he said. 'I am unclean because I have touched it. I must go and bathe in the sea. Then I will come and worship you, and afterwards I will burn my brother's body. Meanwhile, I leave it in your care.'

Chellan left, and the God told his attendant Ganas (goblins) to watch over the body. These Ganas are inclined to be mischievous, and when the God wasn't looking, they gobbled up the body of Gangan.

When Chellan came back from bathing, he reverently worshipped Pillaiyar. He then looked for his brother's body. It was not to be found. Anxiously he demanded it of the God. Pillaiyar called on his goblins to produce it. Terrified, they confessed to what they had done.

Chellan reproached the God for the misdeeds of his attendants. And Pillaiyar felt so much pity for him, that by his divine power he restored dead Gangan's body to Chellan, and brought Gangan to life again.

The two brothers then returned to King Pandya's capital, where Gangan married the princess and became king when her father died.

And so the fourth prophecy was fulfilled:

'For a little while happiness shall follow.'

But there are wise men who say that the lines of the prophecy were wrongly read and understood, and that the whole should run:

'From birth, poverty;
For ten years, captivity;

On the sea-shore, death for a little while;
Happiness shall follow.'

It is the last two lines that are different. And this must be the
correct version, because when happiness came to Gangan it was
not 'for a little while.' When the Goddess of Good Fortune did
arrive, she stayed in his palace for many, many years.

A BATTLE OF WITS

IN a village in northern India there lived a Bania, a merchant whose shop kept the villagers supplied with their everyday necessities.

One day, on his way to a neighbouring town to make some purchases, he met a poor Jat, one of a tribe of farmers who was also going to town to pay the monthly instalment of a debt he owed to the local mahajan, the banker and moneylender.

The debt had actually been incurred by the Jat's great-grandfather and had in the beginning been only fifty rupees; but his great grandfather had been unable to repay it, and in the last fifty years, through interest and compound interest, the amount had grown to five hundred rupees.

The Jat was walking along, wondering if he would ever get out of the clutches of the mahajan, when the Bania caught up with him.

'Good day to you, Chowdhri,' said the Bania, who, though he had a poor opinion of the farmer's intelligence, was always polite to his customers. 'I see you are going to town to pay your instalment to the mahajan. Before long you will have to give up your lands. Can nothing be done to save them?'

'It is too late to do anything, Shahji,' said the Jat. He was much taller and stronger than the Bania; at the same time he was an easy-going, good-natured sort. The Bania thought he was simple-minded.

'Well, let us forget our worries,' said the Bania, 'and pass the time telling stories.'

'A good idea, Shahji! It will make the journey less tiresome. But let there be one condition. No matter how fantastic or silly the story, neither of us must call it untrue. Whoever does so, must pay the other five hundred rupees!'

'Agreed,' said the Bania with a laugh. 'And let me begin my story first. My great-grandfather was the greatest of Banias, and tremendously rich.'

'True, oh Shahji, true!' said the Jat.

'At one time he possessed a fleet of forty ships with which he sailed to China, and traded there in rich jewels and costly silks.'

'True, oh Shahji, true!' said the Jat.

'Well, after making a huge fortune my great-grandfather returned home with many unique and precious things. One was a statue of pure gold which was able to answer any question put to it.'

'True, oh Shahji, true!'

'When my great-grandfather came home, many people came to have their questions answered by his wonderful statue. One day your great-grandfather came with a question. He asked: "Who are the wisest of all men?" The statue replied: "The Banias, of course." Then he asked: "And who are the most foolish?" The statue replied: "The Jats." And then your great-grandfather asked, "Among the Jats, who is the most stupid?" The statue replied: "Why, you are, of course."'

'True, oh Shahji, true,' said the Jat, inwardly resolving to repay the Bania in his own coin.

'My father,' continued the Bania, 'was himself a great traveller, and during a tour of the world he saw many wonders. One day, a mosquito hovering near his ear threatened to bite him. My father, not wishing to kill the mosquito, requested it to leave. The mosquito was amazed at such gentlemanly conduct. It said, "Noble Shahji, you are the greatest man I ever met, and I mean to do you a great service." Saying this, the mosquito opened its mouth, and inside it my father saw a large palace with golden doors and windows. At one of the windows stood the most beautiful princess in the world. At the door of the palace he saw a peasant about to attack the princess. My father, who was very brave, at once jumped into the mouth of the mosquito and entered its stomach. He found it very dark inside.'

'True, oh Shahji, true!' said the Jat.

'Well, after some time my father grew used to the darkness and was able to make out the palace, the princess and the peasant. He at once fell upon the peasant, who happened to be your father. They fought for a year in the stomach of the mosquito. At the end of that time your father was defeated and became my father's servant. My father then married the princess and I was born from the union. But when I was fifteen years old, a heavy rain of boiling water fell on the palace, which collapsed, throwing us into a scalding sea. With great difficulty we swam ashore, where the four of us found ourselves in a kitchen, where a woman was shaking with terror at the sight of us.'

'True, oh Shahji, true!'

'When the woman, who was a cook, realized that we were men and not ghosts, she complained that we had spoilt her soup. "Why did you have to enter my pot of boiling water and frighten me like that?" she complained. We apologized, explaining that for fifteen years we had been living in the belly of a mosquito, and that it was not our fault that we had found ourselves in her cooking pot. "Ah! I remember now," she said. "A little while ago a mosquito bit me on the arm. You must have been injected into my arm, for when I squeezed out the poison, a large black drop fell into the boiling water. I had no idea you were in it!"'

'True, oh Shahji, true!' said the Jat.

'Well, when we left the kitchen we found ourselves in another country, which happened to be our present village. Here we took to shopkeeping. The princess, my mother, died many years ago. That, Chowdhri, is my story. Improve upon it if you can!'

'A very true story,' said the Jat. 'My story; though no less true, is perhaps not as wonderful. But it is perfectly true, every word of it...'

'My great-grandfather was the wealthiest Jat in the village. His noble appearance and great wisdom brought praise from all who met him. At village meetings he was always given the best seat, and when he settled disputes no one questioned his good judgement. In addition, he was of great physical strength, and a terror to the wicked.'

'True, oh Chowdhri, true,' said the Bania.

'There was a time when a great famine came to our village. There was no rain, the rivers and wells dried up, the trees withered away. Birds and beasts died in thousands. When my great-grandfather saw that the village stores had been exhausted, and that the people would die of hunger if something was not done, he called the Jats together and said, "Brother Jats, God Indra is angry with us for some reason, because he has withheld the seasonal rains. But if you do what I tell you, I will supply you all with food until the scarcity is over. I want you to give your fields to me for six months." Without any hesitation the Jats gave my great-grandfather their fields. Then, stripping himself of his clothes, he gave one great heave and lifted the entire village of a thousand acres and placed it on his head!'

'True, oh Chowdhri, true!' exclaimed the Bania.

'Then my great-grandfather, carrying the village on his head, searched for rain...'

'Wherever there was rain he took the village, so that the rainwater fell on the fields and collected in the wells. Then he told the Jats (who were of course still in the village on his head) to plough their land and sow their seed. The crops that came up had never been so wonderful, and the wheat and the maize rose to such a height that they touched the clouds.'

'True, oh Chowdhri, true,' said the Bania.

'Then my great-grandfather returned to his country and placed the village in its proper place. The farmers reaped a record harvest that year. Ever grain of corn was as big as your head.'

'True, oh Chowdhri, true,' said the Bania, annoyed at the comparison but anxious not to lose his wager. By this time, they had reached the outskirts of the town, but the Jat had not finished his story.

'At that time your great-grandfather was a very poor man,' said the Jat, 'and mine, who had made huge profits from his wonderful harvest, employed him as a servant to weigh out the grain for the customers.'

'True, oh Chowdhri, true,' said the Bania with a sour look. 'Being a blockhead, your ancestor often made mistakes for which he would receive thrashings from my great-grandfather.'

'True, oh Chowdhri, true!'

By this time they had entered the shop of the mahajan to whom the Jat owed money. Bidding the banker good morning, they sat down on the floor in front of him. But the Jat, without speaking to the banker, continued his story.

'Well, Shahji, after my great-grandfather sold his harvest he discharged your great-grandfather. But, before he went, your ancestor asked mine for a loan of fifty rupees, which was generously given to him.'

'True, oh Chowdhri, true!' said the Bania.

'Very good,' said the Jat, raising his voice so that the mahajan could also hear them. 'Your ancestor did not repay that debt. Nor did your grandfather, or your father, repay the debt. Neither have you repaid it up to this time.'

'True, oh Chowdhri, true!'

'Now that sum of fifty rupees, with interest and compound interest, amounts to exactly five hundred rupees, which is the sum you owe me!'

'True, oh Chowdhri, true!'

'So, as you have admitted the debt before the mahajan, kindly pay the amount to him so that I may have my lands released.'

This placed the Bania in a dilemma. He had admitted a debt before a third party. If he said that it was merely a story, and completely untrue, he would have to pay the Jat five hundred rupees according to the terms of the wager. If he said it was true, he would have to pay the amount to the mahajan. Either way he was the loser.

So the Bania paid up, and never again did he belittle the intelligence of his Jat neighbours.

THE GHOST AND THE IDIOT

In a village near Agra there lived a family, which was under the special protection of a Munjia, a ghost who lived in a peepul tree. The ghost had attached himself to this particular family and showed his fondness for its members by throwing stones, bones, night-soil and other rubbish at them, and making hideous noises, terrifying them at every opportunity. Under his patronage, the family dwindled away. One by one they died, the only survivor being an idiot boy, whom the ghost did not bother because he felt it beneath his dignity to do so.

But in an Indian village, marriage (like birth and death) must come to all, and it was not long before the neighbours began to make plans for the marriage of the idiot.

After a meeting of the village elders it was decided, first, that the idiot should be married; and second, that he should be married to a shrew of a girl who had passed the age of twenty without finding a suitor!

The shrew and the idiot were soon married off, then left to manage for themselves. The poor idiot had no means of earning a living and had to resort to begging. He had barely been able to support himself before, and now his wife was an additional burden. The first thing she did when she entered the house was to give him a box on the ear and send him out to bring something home for dinner.

The poor fellow went from door to door, but nobody gave him anything, because the same people who had arranged the marriage were annoyed that he had not given them a wedding feast. In the evening, when he returned home empty-handed, his wife cried out: 'Are you back, you lazy idiot? Why have you been so long, and what have you brought for me?'

When she found he hadn't even a paisa, she flew into a rage and, removing his head-cloth, tossed it into the peepul tree. Then, taking up her broom, she belaboured her husband until he fled from the house.

But the shrew's anger had not yet been assuaged. Seeing her husband's head-cloth in the peepul tree, she began venting her rage on the tree-trunk, accompanying her blows with the most shocking abuse. The ghost who lived in the tree was sensitive to both her blows and her language. Alarmed that her terrible curses might put an end to him, he took to his heels and left the tree in which he had lived for so many years.

Riding on a whirlwind, the ghost soon caught up with the idiot who was still fleeing down the road away from the village.

'Not so fast, brother!' cried the ghost. 'Desert your wife, by all means, but don't abandon your old family ghost! That shrew has driven me out of the peepul tree. What powerful arms she has—and what a vile tongue! She has made brothers of us brothers in misfortune. And so we must seek our fortunes together! But first promise me you will not return to your wife.' The idiot made this promise very willingly, and together they journeyed until they reached a large city.

Before they entered the city, the ghost said, 'Now listen, brother. If you follow my advice, your fortune is made. In this city there are two very beautiful girls, one the daughter of a king and the other the daughter of a rich money-lender. I will go and possess the daughter of the king, and when he finds her possessed by a spirit he will try every sort of remedy but with no effect. Meanwhile, you must walk daily through the streets in the dress of a sadhu—one who has renounced the world—and when the king comes and asks you if you can cure his daughter, undertake to do so and make your own terms. As soon as I see you, I shall leave the girl. Then I shall go and possess the daughter of the money-lender. But do not go near her, because I am in love with the girl and do not intend giving her up! If you come near her, I shall break your neck.'

The ghost went off on his whirlwind, while the idiot entered the city on his own and found a bed at the local inn for pilgrims.

The following day everyone in the city was agog with the news that the king's daughter was dangerously ill. Physicians of all sorts came and went, and all pronounced the girl incurable. The king was on the verge of a nervous breakdown. He offered half his fortune to anyone who could cure his beautiful and only child. The idiot, having smeared himself with dust and ashes like a sadhu, began walking the streets, reciting religious verses.

The people were struck by the idiot's appearance. They took him for a wise and holy man, and reported him to the king, who immediately came into the city, prostrated himself before the idiot, and begged him to cure his daughter. After a show of modesty and reluctance, the idiot was persuaded to accompany the king back to the palace, and the girl was brought before him.

Her hair was dishevelled, her teeth were chattering, and her eyes almost starting from their sockets. She howled and cursed and tore at her clothes. The idiot confronted her and recited a few meaningless spells. And the ghost, recognizing him, cried out in terror; 'I'm going, I'm going! I'm on my way!'

'Give me a sign that you have gone,' demanded the idiot.

'As soon as I leave the girl,' said the ghost, 'you will see that mango tree uprooted. That is the sign I'll give.'

A few minutes later the mango tree came crashing down. The girl recovered from her fit and seemed unaware of what had happened. The news of her miraculous cure spread through the city, and the idiot became an object of veneration and wonder. The king kept his word and gave him half his fortune; and so began a period of happiness and prosperity for the idiot.

A few weeks later the ghost took possession of the moneylender's daughter, with whom he was in love. Seeing his daughter take leave of her senses, the money-lender sent for the highly respected idiot and offered him a great sum of money to cure his daughter. But remembering the ghost's warning, the idiot refused. The money-lender was enraged and sent his henchmen to bring the idiot to him by force; and the idiot was dragged along to the rich man's house.

As soon as the ghost saw his old companion, he cried out in a rage: 'Idiot, why have you broken our agreement and come here? Now I will have to break your neck!'

But the idiot, whose reputation for wisdom had actually helped to make him wiser, said, 'Brother ghost, I have not come to trouble you but to tell you a terrible piece of news. Old friend and protector, we must leave this city soon. She has come here— my dreaded wife—to torment us both, and to drag us back to the village. She is on her way and will be here any minute!'

When the ghost heard this, he cried out, 'Oh no, oh no! If she has come, then we must go!'

And breaking down the walls and doors of the house, the ghost gathered himself up into a little whirlwind and went scurrying out of the city to look for a vacant peepul tree.

The money-lender, delighted that his daughter had been freed of the evil influence, embraced the idiot and showered presents on him. And in due course the idiot married the money-lender's beautiful daughter, inherited his wealth and debtors, and became the richest and most successful money-lender in the city.

BLUE BEARD

An Old Tale from the French

Think of it! A man rich as a prince, of fine upstanding presence and commanding manner; a man of great moment in Baghdad!

Think of it again! A man cursed by nature with a beard that was quite blue, from the roots of the hairs to their very tips!

To be sure, he had three alternatives in the matter. First, he might shave it off, thus avoiding earthly ugliness while renouncing all hope of a place in Paradise; secondly, he might marry a scold, and so become prematurely grey; and last, he might keep his blue beard and remain the ugliest man in all the world. There was no other alternative, for the beard was so deadly blue that no dye could touch it.

He had staked his chances on the second point: he had married, and more than once; but, although his wives had disappeared mysteriously, his blue beard still remained, as blue as ever. How it was that he had ever found any woman blind enough to marry him it is difficult to imagine, for he was so frightfully ugly that most women at sight of him ran away screaming, and hid in the cellar. But it is only fair to say that Blue Beard had such a way with him that, given two hours' start, he could snap his fingers at any rival.

Now it so happened that, in his neighbourhood, there lived a lady of quality, who had two sons and two daughters; and, in his walks abroad, Blue Beard often met the two girls, and soon fell into the lowest depths of love. Both were adorable, and he really could not decide which one he preferred. Always in exquisite doubt on the point, he finally approached the mother and asked her for the hand of one of her daughters, leaving the choice to her. And she, like a wise woman, said nothing, but simply introduced Blue Beard to Anne and Fatima, and left the rest to nature and their own fancies.

But neither Anne nor Fatima fell in love with their admirer at first sight. His beard was so blue that they could not endure it, and, between them, they led him a dance. Neither was inclined to marry a man with a beard like that, and, what made matters worse, they soon learned that he had already been married several times, and that his wives had disappeared mysteriously. This was rather disconcerting, and each was angling for a brother-in-law rather than a husband.

But, as already stated, Blue Beard had a way with him. He did not expect to be accepted at first asking. Indeed, when he proposed, first to one and then to the other, they both said, 'Oh! You must see father about it'. Now Blue Beard knew very well that their father, having led a very wicked life, was dead and gone; and, as he pondered over it, stroking his beard the while, he began to realize what they meant when they said, 'You must see father about it'.

But Blue Beard did not despair, he merely altered his plan. He invited the whole family, with some of their chosen friends, to one of his country houses, where he gave them the time of their lives. Hunting, hawking, shooting with the bow, or fishing for goldfish in the ponds, they enjoyed themselves to the full especially in the evenings, when they were rowed upon the lake to the sound of beautiful music, and made moonlight excursions to some of Blue Beard's ruined castles, of which he possessed quite a number. Whatever the nature of the day's pleasure party, the night hours were taken up with banqueting, dancing, or some other form of revelry, until such a late hour that Blue Beard said to himself, 'Only wait till I marry one of them, then we shall see who is master.' For the present he was content to take their pranks in good part. When he found himself trying in vain to get into an apple-pie bed he merely laughed; when he found his pillow stuffed with prickly cactus, or the sleeves and legs of his garments stitched up so that he could not put them on, he swore merrily and fell more deeply in love than ever. One day they cut down the stem of an aloe that was about to flower—a thing which happened only once in every hundred years. The head gardener, who had been listening every day for the loud report with which the aloe blossoms burst their sheath, was heartbroken when he saw what had been done; but Blue Beard consoled him by raising his wages, saying that in a hundred years' time, when every one was bald, the plant might blossom again—what did it matter? In fact, things went so smoothly, and everything in the garden was so very lovely, that the younger daughter, Fatima, being the more poetical and impressionable of the two, began quietly to think what a splendid beard their host's would be if it were not so blue. From this—for you know that love is colour-blind—she began to see the beard in a different light. Like a dutiful and affectionate daughter she spoke to her mother upon the point.

'Mother,' she said, 'it may be only my fancy, but I really think his beard has changed a little in colour during the last few days. Perhaps it's the country air, I don't know; but it doesn't seem to me quite so blue, after all.'

'My darling child,' replied the mother, 'it is strange that you should have mentioned that. I had also noticed it, but, thinking my sight was failing me, I feared that old age was creeping on, and so held my tongue on the matter.'

'That settles it, dear mother. Sooner than believe that you are growing old and your sight is failing I prefer to believe that what we have both noticed is an actual fact. But mind you, though there is a slight change, it is still horribly blue, mother.'

'Yes, dear; but blue's a very nice colour. It's lucky to some people. The eyes of the Goddess of Love were blue; the sky above is blue; the bird of Paradise is blue; the deep sea is blue. Press your thumbs on your eyes and what do you see? Blue—the deepest blue imaginable: it is the light of the mind and soul burning in your head, dear; and that is why poets and singers are so found of blue.'

'Then you think—'

'Think? I know, child. Besides, a man with a blue beard is different from all other men; and besides, again, in the dark all beards are black.'

'But even in the light, dear mother, you think it is changing— just a little?'

'Yes, my darling, I do. And the reason I know full well. He has fallen in love, dear; and I think I know with whom. And love can work wonders. Just as grief can turn black hair grey, so can love turn a blue beard—'

'Not grey, mother. Say a greyish blue.'

'I was going to say a bluish grey. But there—if this worthy gentleman suffers from an affliction—which, mind you, I am far from allowing—what could be sweeter in a woman than to pity him? And pity, my darling, sometimes leads to love.'

Fatima then sought her sister Anne, and told her what was on her mind. 'Oh, well,' said Anne when she had heard all about the wonderful change, 'your having discovered it now saves me the trouble of finding it out later on. Not only do I thank you,

Fatima, I congratulate you.'

Greatly relieved by her mother's and her sister's attitude, Fatima decked herself out in her best, and waited for Blue Beard to come and find her, which she felt sure he would do. And she was right. That very evening Blue Beard led her aside from the others into the garden, where the moon was shining and the nightingales singing. And there he spoke soft words to her, and wooed and won her for his wife. As soon as they returned to town the wedding was celebrated, and there were great rejoicings over the happy event.

Now, shortly after the honeymoon was over, Blue Beard was called away into the country on matters of urgent importance, which would occupy his attention for at least six weeks. And when Fatima, on hearing this, pouted and began to cry, he sought to console her by suggesting that she should amuse herself among her friends during his absence.

'See now, my dear,' he said, 'these keys will unlock all the doors for you so that you shall want for nothing. These two are the keys of the store-chambers, and these others open the strong rooms where the gold and silver plate is kept. These here are the keys to my money chests, and these smaller ones fit the locks of my jewel coffers. But this little one here'—he separated a curious little key from the others and showed it to her—'is the key of the little room with the iron door at the end of the great corridor. Do what you will with all the rest, but, I warn you, open not that door. Now, I have trusted you with everything: if you disobey me in this one little matter you will incur my gravest displeasure.'

'That will I never do,' said Fatima as she took the keys from his hand. And she meant it at the time. Blue Beard kissed her, embracing her fondly. Then he entered his coach and was driven away.

Fatima, in her grand home, eagerly welcomed the change of

holding high revelry and playing hostess to her friends. They all came running at her invitation, and were immediately shown over the great house. Rooms, cupboards, wardrobes, closets, cabinets and presses were opened by the aid of keys on the bunch, and they went into ecstasies over the wonderful treasures the house contained. There were magnificent pictures, tapestries, costly silk hangings, gold and silver ornaments, the loveliest soft carpets, and, best of all, gold-framed looking glasses reaching from floor to ceiling. These last, which cast one's reflection taller and fairer than the original inlooker, were the subject of long and careful admiration. All spoke with rapture of the splendid luxury of the place, and congratulated Fatima on her great good fortune.

'For my part,' said one, 'if my husband could give me such a magnificent house as this, I would not trouble about the colour of his beard.'

'You're right,' said another. 'Why, for half this grandeur I would marry a man even if his beard were all the colours of the rainbow, especially if he went away and left me the keys of the whole house.'

'The whole house,' thought Fatima, 'nay, this little key here he has forbidden me to use. I wonder why!'

But he had been so stern about it—and his beard got very blue when he was angry—that Fatima put her curiosity away, and continued to entertain her guests. Still, the temptation to slip away and open that forbidden door returned again and again; but always she said to herself, 'Nay; I have the run of the whole house beside: is it a great matter that I am forbidden one pokey little room at the end of a dark corridor?' Then, having triumphed for the twentieth time, she fell at last the more easily—at least she fell to this extent, that she slipped away from her guests and ran along the corridor, just to go and take a peep at the door.

There was nothing unusual about the door. It was of plain,

solid iron, and the keyhole was very small. She wondered if the little key would fit it. She tried, and found that it went in quite easily; yet, remembering her promise, she would not turn it, but pulled it out again and tore herself away. But, after all, she could not see what possible harm there could be in opening a small room like that and just having one look inside. Besides, if her husband had been really serious he would have kept the key himself and not given it to her with the others. To be sure, he was a kind, indulgent husband, and would not be so very angry; and then, again, he need never know that she had opened the door.

With thoughts like these passing quickly in her mind she hesitated, paused, and finally turned again to the door. Her disobedient hands trembled as she selected the key a second time, detached it from the bunch, and inserted it in the lock. In another moment she had turned it and pushed the heavy door open.

At first, as the shutters were closed, she could see nothing; but gradually her eyes became accustomed to the dim light and she saw that the floor was of porphyry—at all events, it was red. Then, as she shaded her eyes from the light creeping through the chinks of the shutters, and peered more closely, she discovered to her horror that what she had taken for porphyry was nothing of the kind—it was blood! Here it had clotted in dark crimson pools, and there it had run in little streams along the irregular stone floor. Quickly she traced those streams to their source by the opposite wall, where, as she raised her eyes, she discerned seven dark forms hanging feet downwards from seven spikes driven through their necks into the masonry.

Her first impulse was to flee from the spot—then there came a dreadful thought, and she stayed. Whose bodies were those hanging in the forbidden cupboard? She took a step forward and inspected them more closely. Yes, they were women, and they had been young and beautiful. O horror of horrors! Could it be true? Were those the bodies of Blue Beard's wives, who had disappeared, one after another, so mysteriously? There they hung, spiked through the neck, their feet dangling above pools of their life's blood—mute evidence of foul murder.

As Fatima stood gazing at the scene before her, her eyes dilated with fear, and, her breath coming in gasps, the little key fell from her fingers and clinked upon the floor. The sound recalled her to her senses, and she picked the key up hastily. Then she turned and rushed out; and, having locked the door—no easy feat with such trembling hands—she ran upstairs, her face as pale as death. She thought to escape and regain her composure in her own room, but, when she arrived there, she found it full of her guests, who were so busy admiring its luxurious appointments that her pallor went unnoticed. One by one, however, perceiving that she was tired, they melted away, promising to come again on the morrow—unless her husband was expected to return. It was evident they feared him; so did she, now.

At last they were all gone, and, as soon as she was left alone, she bethought her of the key and drew it from her pocket. What was her horror to observe the dull red stain of blood upon it, which she had not noticed when she picked it up from the blood-smeared floor of the dreadful chamber. Quickly she seized the nearest rag, thinking to wipe off the stain; but, rub as she might, it would not come off. As she scoured and polished without result, terror slowly grew on her face. 'Alas!' she cried, 'There is Blue Magic in this. Now I know my husband has consorted with fiends: his beard for one thing, this bewitched key for another. If I am not mistaken, nothing will remove the stain of foul murder from this key.'

Nevertheless, she bethought herself of many things: of sand, and pumice, and strong acid, and she tried them all upon the key; but though she wore the metal away by hard rubbing, the bloodstain still remained, for, being a magic key, it had absorbed the blood of Blue Beard's victims, and was saturated through and through with it.

She was just beginning to realize that the task was hopeless when she heard the rumble of wheels, but she still went on polishing the key, for, whatever coach was approaching, she assured herself it could not be her husband's—thank heaven, he was not due to return yet for six weeks, and by that time she might contrive to have a new key made, exactly like the old one. But presently, when the coach drew up at the gate, and the horns sounded in her husband's style and manner, she started up with a cry of dismay, and her knees trembled with sudden fright.

Her first care was to hide the key in her bosom; then she ran out, but, for very fear, could get no farther than the head of the main stairway, where she stood clutching the stair-rail, and quaking in every limb. There, in the hall below, stood Blue Beard giving some final orders to the coachman. With a quick movement he turned, and, looking up, perceived her standing irresolute.

'Yes, it is I, my darling,' he called up gaily as he advanced to the foot of the stairs. 'Some letters reached me on the road, showing me that my long journey was unnecessary. So, you see, I have returned to your arms.'

By this time Fatima was tottering down the stairs, bent on giving him a fitting welcome; for, though she feared him more than anything else, she must try not to show it. 'Seven of them!' she kept saying to herself, as she gripped the balustrade, 'And seven and one are eight! And I have a throat as well as they, as sure as iron spikes have points.'

There was only a dim light in the hall, so that Blue Beard could not see her trembling condition; and if, when she greeted him, he felt that her body was quaking, he was fond enough to put it down to joy at his unexpected return. And Fatima, taking cover in this, behaved in an excited manner, like one so delighted to see her husband back again that she did not know what she was doing. She ran hither and thither, ordering this and that to be done, and then countermanding the orders, doing this or that herself, and then immediately undoing it again—behaving, in short, like one demented with excitement, until Blue Beard smiled and stroked his beard, and thought she was a wonderful little bundle of delight.

And so, through such artfulness long sustained, it transpired that the question of the keys did not arise all that night, nor, indeed, until late the following day, when, as ominous as a thunderclap, came a summons from Blue Beard that Fatima should attend him immediately on the terrace. With a wildly beating heart she hastened to answer the summons.

'I want my keys,' he said in the usual manner of a man. 'Where are they?'

'The keys?—Oh yes, the keys. I—I will go and fetch them immediately.'

Fatima ran off, and you can imagine her thoughts and feelings as she went. Blue Beard remained—he was always a grim figure—standing as she had left him—just waiting: his thoughts and feelings were in his beard.

Presently Fatima returned, purposely out of breath in order to hide whatever confusion she might feel, and handed the bunch of keys to her husband. He took them without a word, looked at them carefully, and then slowly turned his eyes upon her. 'The key of the room at the end of the corridor,' he said grimly, 'it is not here: where is it?'

'The key of the—oh, you mean the key of the—'

'I mean the key of the—; yes, that's what I mean. Where is it?'

'Oh! I remember now. You said I was not to use it; so, to

make sure, I took it off the bunch and put it away in a drawer of my dressing-table. I will run and fetch it.'

'Do,' said Blue Beard, and, while she ran off, he stood there looking for all the world like a blue thundercloud before the lightning comes.

Once out of sight Fatima paused to collect her wits. Then, having made up her mind, she ran twice up and down stairs, and finally rejoined her husband, panting heavily.

'It is not there,' she cried in dismay. 'I put it in my jewel case—of that I'm sure—but now it's gone. Who can have taken it?'

'Go look again,' replied Blue Beard, dangerously calm.

She ran away again, and again came running back. 'No,' she said, 'it is not there. Who can have—?'

'Silence, madam!' broke in Blue Beard. 'That was no ordinary key; and something tells me it is in your bosom now.' And, with this, he gathered her shrinking form in his rough arm, and with a rougher hand searched for, and found—the key!

'So!' he said. 'You lied to me. And—what is this? How came this blood upon the key?'

Fatima was very pale, and trembling like an aspen leaf. 'I do not know,' she replied. 'Perhaps—'

'Perhaps nothing!' roared Blue Beard in a terrible voice. 'Madam! Your face tells me you are guilty. You have presumed to disobey me; to enter that room at the end of the corridor. Yes, madam; and, since you would sooner indulge your fancy for that room than obey my commands, you shall go there and stay as long as you like. Seven and one are eight, madam!'

'Mercy! Mercy!' cried Fatima, flinging herself at Blue Beard's feet. 'Do what you will with me, but do not put me in that room.'

She looked up sobbing, imploring his forgiveness; and, if a woman's beauty in despair could have melted a heart of stone, the sight of her would have melted his. But it will not astonish you to know that his heart was as flinty as his beard was blue, and Fatima realized this as she looked again at his terrible face.

'I have said it, madam,' he replied to her pleadings. 'None can disobey me and live. Prepare, then, for death.'

'Then,' said she, her imploring eyes brimming with tears, 'you will give me a little time to prepare? If I must die, I must say my prayers.'

'Ten minutes will suffice for that. Not a second more.'

Fatima hurried away towards her own room, but on the way she met her sister Anne, who was looking for her.

'Oh! Dear Anne,' sobbed Fatima, as she embraced her sister, 'Ask me no questions; there is no time. My husband has returned, and, because I disobeyed him, he has threatened to kill me. Oh! where are my brothers? If they were only here!'

'They are on the way hither,' said Anne quickly. 'They were delayed, but promised to follow me very soon.'

'Then run, dear sister, if you love me; run to the top of the tower, and, if you can see them coming, make a sign to them to hasten; for in ten minutes I must die.'

Quickly Anne ran up and up until she reached the roof of the tower; and Fatima, standing at the foot, called up to her, 'Sister Anne! Dear sister Anne! Do you see any one coming?'

And Anne answered her: 'I see naught but dust a-blowing, naught but the green grass growing.'

Presently, Fatima called up again: 'Sister Anne, can you see no one coming?'

'Nay, I see naught but dust a-blowing, naught but the green grass growing.'

Fatima, in despair, continued to call again and again, but always the same answer came down from the roof of the tower. And so the ten minutes ran out, and Fatima wrung her hands and groaned.

Meanwhile, Blue Beard, having sharpened his sword, was trying its edge on the greensward of the terrace below. Fully satisfied with it, he strode into the house, and, standing at the foot of the stairs, shouted, 'Madam, your time is up. Come down at once!'

'One moment—just one moment,' she replied, then called softly to her sister: 'Anne, sister Anne, do you see any one coming?'

'Nay, naught but dust a-blowing, naught but the green grass growing.'

'Madam,' roared Blue Beard, 'if you do not come down quickly, I will come up and drag you down.'

'I am coming,' she replied; and again she called softly to Anne: 'Sister Anne, do you see any one coming?'

'Sister, I see a great cloud of dust.'

'Raised by galloping horses?' '

Alas! Nay, it is but a flock of sheep.'

'Will you come down?' bellowed Blue Beard, 'Or by—'

'I am coming in another moment.' Then to Anne: 'Sister Anne, can you see anybody coming?'

'Yonder I see—God be praised—I see two knights in armour, riding fast... Yes, they are my brothers... I am waving my kerchief to them... They see me... They spur and hasten... Sister, they will soon be here.'

Then Blue Beard stamped his foot and roared out so terribly that he made the whole house tremble. At this his poor wife, wholly fascinated by terror, crept down to her doom. Her face was stained with tears, her long hair was dishevelled; she flung herself at his feet and besought him to take pity on her.

'Pity!' he thundered, 'I have no pity. You must die!' He seized her by the hair and twisted her head back to expose her beautiful throat; then, flourishing his sword, he went on: 'This is my last word on the abominable crime of curiosity as practised by women.

By that detestable vice misfortune and grief came into the world, and we owe our present state of evil to the first woman, whose daughters greatly resemble her in that peculiar gift of prying into matters forbidden...' And so he continued to harangue his poor wife, grasping her hair with one hand while he flourished his great sword with the other.

When at length he paused for want of words to describe the horrible crime he was about to meet with punishment, Fatima wailed, 'O sir! Wilt thou punish me before I have recommended myself to Heaven? One moment, I implore thee, while I turn my soul to God.'

'Nay, thy prayers are said.' And he raised his sword to strike. But the sword remained in air, as Blue Beard, startled by a loud battering at the gate, turned his head. Then, as the gate was burst in, and two knights came running with drawn swords, he loosed his hold upon Fatima, who sank in a huddled heap like one already dead. Turning quickly, Blue Beard fled, but the two brothers were hot upon his heels; and, after a rapid chase through the house and garden, they came up with him just as he reached the steps of the main porch. There they ran their swords through and through his body, and left him dead in a pool of blood.

When Fatima opened her eyes and saw her two brothers and her sister Anne bending over her, she thanked heaven for her deliverance. With a sword all dripping red, one brother pointed towards the porch, and Fatima gave a deep sigh of relief. She knew, and was satisfied to know, she was a widow.

Now, as Blue Beard had no children by any of his wives, his sole surviving wife became mistress of all that had been his. All his vast estates and treasures came into her possession, and she was young and beautiful into the bargain. The first thing she did was to purchase commissions for her two brothers in the army; next, she bestowed a splendid estate and a large sum of money upon her sister Anne as a wedding present on the occasion of her marrying the young man of her choice. Then Fatima fell in love with, and married, a worthy gentleman who adored her, and these two lived out their lives in one continuous hour of happiness.

His beard was black, and, when at length it grew grey, and then silvery white, she only loved him all the more. Even in the first year of her marriage she had quite forgotten the dark cloud cast upon her early life by that terrible man, Blue Beard; and ever afterwards she never had the slightest cause or reason to remember him.

SINDBAD THE SAILOR

A Tale from the Thousand and One Nights

O King of the Age, as thou biddest me retell the strangest
adventure of Sindbad the Sailor in all his O marvellous
voyages, I will name it without hesitation: it is that of Sindbad's
fifth voyage, wherein he was in fearful peril from that great bird,
the rukh, and afterwards was ridden almost to the point of death
by the Old Man of the Sea.

But first let me call to thy recollection how Sindbad the Sailor
came to tell his story to Sindbad the Landsman, for herein lies
much meaning, O King.

In the time of the Caliph Harun-er-Rashid, in the palmy
days of Baghdad, there lived and slaved a poor, discontented
porter, whose moments of rest and leisure were most pleasantly
occupied in grumbling at his hard lot. Others lived in luxury
and splendour while he bore heavy burdens for a pittance. There
was no justice in the world, said he, when some were born in
the lap of wealth, and others toiled a lifetime for the price of a
decent burial.

This discontented porter would run apace with his burden to
gain time for a rest upon the doorstep of some mansion of the rich,
where, a master in contrasts, he would draw comparisons between
his own lot and that of the rich man dwelling within. Loudly

would he call on destiny to mark the disparity, the incongruity, the injustice of the thing; and not until he had drunk deep at the fountain of discontent would he take up his burden and trudge on, greatly refreshed.

One day, in pursuance of this strange mode of recreation, he chanced to select the doorstep of a wealthy merchant named Sindbad the Sailor, and there, through the open window, he heard as it were the chink of endless gold. The song, the music, the dance, the laughter of the guests—all seemed to shine with the light of jewels and the lustre of golden bars. Immediately he began to revel in his favourite woe. He wrung his hands and cried aloud: 'Allah! Can such things be? Look at me, toiling all day for a piece of barley bread; and then look on him who knows no toil, yet eateth peacocks' tongues from golden dishes, and drinketh the wine of Paradise from a jewelled cup. What bath has he taken to obtain from thee a lot so agreeable? And what have I done to deserve a life so wretched?'

As one who flings back a difficult question, and then bangs the door behind him, so the porter rose and shouldered his burden to continue his way, when a servant came running from within, saying that his master had sharp ears and had invited the porter into his presence for a fuller hearing of his woes.

As soon as the porter came before the wealthy owner of the house, seated among his guests and surrounded by the utmost luxury and magnificence, he was greeted with the question: 'What is thy name?' 'My name is Sindbad,' replied the porter, greatly abashed. At this the host clapped his hands and laughed loudly. 'Knowest thou that my name is also Sindbad?' he cried. 'But I am Sindbad the Sailor, and I have a mind to call thee Sindbad the Landsman, for, as thou lovest a contrast, so do I.'

'True,' said the porter, 'I have never been upon the sea.'

'Then, Sindbad the Landsman,' was the quick rejoinder, 'thou hast no right to complain of thy hard lot. Come, be seated, and, when thou hast refreshed thyself with food and wine, I will relate to thee what at present I have told no man—the tale of my perils and hardships on the seas and in other lands—in order to show you that the great wealth I possess was not acquired without excessive toil and terrible danger. I have made seven voyages: the first thou shalt hear presently—nay, if thou wilt accept my hospitality for seven days, I will tell thee the history of one each day.'

Thus it was, O King, that Sindbad the Sailor, surrounded by a multitude of listeners, came to tell the story of his voyages to Sindbad the Landsman. Now on the fifth day he spoke as follows:

'Having sworn that my fourth voyage should be my last, I dwelt in the bosom of my family for many months in the utmost joy and happiness. But soon my heart grew restless in my bosom, and I longed again for the perils of the sea, and the adventures found only in other lands. Moreover, I had become inspired of a new ambition to possess a ship of my own in which to sail afar, and even to greater profit than on my former voyages.

'I arose, therefore, and gathered together in Baghdad many bales of rich merchandise, and departed for the city of El-Basrah, where, in the river's mouth, I soon selected a splendid vessel. I purchased this and secured a master and a crew, over whom I set my own trusty servants. Then, together with a goodly company of merchants as passengers, their bales and mine being placed in the hold, I set sail.

'Fair weather favoured us as we passed from island to island, bartering everywhere for gain, as merchants do, until at length we came to an island which seemed never to have known the fretful heel of man. Here we landed, and, almost immediately, on sweeping our gaze over the interior, we espied a strange thing, on which all our attention and wonder soon became centred.

'There in the distance shone beneath the sun a great white dome. Loud was the talk among us as to the meaning of this. Some said the island could not be uninhabited since a mosque was built upon it; others contended that, as the island was uninhabited, the structure could not be a mosque. A third party, cooling their minds in the shade of the trees, preferred idly that it was probably some huge white rock smoothed and rounded by wind and weather; yet even these, when the discussion became heated, were constrained by curiosity to follow as we bent our steps inland to discover what this strange object really was.

'As we drew nearer and nearer, the wind-and-weather merchants lost in countenance what they gained in speed, for the mystery deepened; it was very clear that no mere wind and weather could have fashioned such a perfect, glistening dome. Nearer still, and then we all ran our utmost, and arrived breathless at the base of the marvellous structure. Gigantic and perfect in form, this must be some wonderful dome built to the glory of Allah, and fashioned in such a way that, with its lower half embedded in earth and its upper half rising in the air, it typified at once the division and the union of heaven and earth. A learned merchant of our company—one who had travelled greatly in the further realms of Ind—raised his voice and assured us that the object represented the mysterious Hiranyagarbha—the Egg of All Things; whereupon another, to test this theory in derision, struck violently with his hatchet upon the shell of this supposed egg. 'If this be the egg of Hiranya—something,' he shouted, 'let us get to the yolk!'

'Following his words, and his blow, the strangest thing happened. The great dome seemed to shake itself as if something within it had awakened to life. We stood in awe and waited. Then, as a chicken comes forth out of its shell, there came forth, with a terrific rending of the dome, a mighty fledgling having the aspect of that monstrous bird, the rukh, which, when grown, darkens the sky with its wings.

"'It is indeed the young of the rukh," I cried, for well I knew the bird. "Beware!"

'At first we were terrified beyond measure, but soon some among us, seeing the helplessness of the creature, set upon it with their hatchets, and though I pleaded with them to forbear, it was quickly slain and dismembered.

"'Whoe!" I cried. "Ye have slain the offspring of the rukh, and, as the time of hatching was near, the parents will come, and there will be trouble."

'But they heeded my words so little that they roasted and ate the choicest parts of the young rukh and left the remains as a sign of contempt. I, who live to tell the tale, O Landsman, did not eat. In vain, I entreated them to conceal all traces of their foul crime, even as they had concealed the choicest portions in their capacious stomachs. In vain, I told them what I had learnt by costly peril at the hands of the giant rukh, foretelling the dire vengeance of those fierce monsters of the sky. Indeed, from the experiences of a former voyage, as you know, I had every reason to fear them. But the merchants, smacking their lips at the memory of their repast, laughed in my face. "We have dined," they said, "and your fearsome rukhs cannot touch us." To this I returned no word, but a stern face; for I knew the power of the rukh.

'We returned towards the ship, but we had no sooner reached the seashore when we saw the master making signs of wild alarm. Shouting loudly to us to make all haste he pointed towards the horizon. He had sailed those seas before, and he knew, as did I, the sign of a terrible danger. There in the distance were two black clouds, growing rapidly larger.

"'A storm!" cried some among us.

"'Nay, nay," I answered. "I would it were, even a twofold

storm. Storms come not so. Yonder come the rukh and his mate to attend the hatching of their young. Aboard! aboard! We may yet escape."

'As soon as I had given this warning there WAS hurry and scurry among the merchants. The flesh of the young rukh seemed to have turned within them, and it now cried out for vengeance. With all haste we made our way on board the ship.

'"What have ye done?" cried the master in alarm.

'They were silent.

'"They have roasted and eaten the young of the rukh," I said. The master wrung his hands and his face blanched. Then he sprang to action.

'"All sail! All sail!" he cried out. "Woe be on us if we escape not quickly. They know not yet, but when they learn they will rest not until—"

'Instantly the crew leapt to the ropes, while the merchants stood around in terror, regarding the two black clouds as they drew rapidly towards us, side by side. Now they loomed nearer as monstrous birds, and presently they passed overhead, darkening the sky as they craned their gigantic necks and looked down upon us with suspicion.

'With the utmost speed the ship was put upon her way, the while we watched the rukhs hover and settle inland. We were already speeding fast for the open sea when we saw them rise and circle in the air, heard their hoarse complaint and clamour for vengeance, and noted their swift swoop towards the rocky heights of the interior. We gave a sigh of relief. We thought we had escaped, so well did the breeze serve us; but we had forgotten, or did not yet know, the power of wings.

'Soon there arose from the far heights of the island two gigantic shapes. As they moved towards us they grew bigger and bigger, and now we heard the beating of their wings, ever louder and louder on our ears. They were coming, the rukhs, to wreak vengeance; and, now we saw it with fear, in the talons of each was a granite crag torn from the bedrock of the island. Their purpose was as plain as it was terrible.

'We cowered as they drew overhead. They circled round the ship, each clutching its mighty rock and giving forth cries of rage and fury. Now they hovered above us, and one let go of his missile of destruction. Our steersman, bent on taking the vessel this way and then that, evaded the falling crag, which fell a caster's throw astern. The ship danced high on the mountain waves raised by the falling mass, and then fell as deep into the watery valleys between them. We thought our time had come, but it was not yet, though it was soon to be. No sooner had we come to rest on a level tide than the other rukh hovered above us and dropped its crag. It struck the ship in the middle and split it to pieces.

'In that moment all was a swirl of confusion. The crash of the rock, the cries of the giant birds, the wash of the waves on my ears—these were the last things I knew. It seems to me that I gripped some wreckage, and, lying thereupon in a swoon, was borne onwards by the tide to the shores of an island; for, when I awoke to life, I found myself on a sandy slope, with my head on the high-water mark and my feet against the stranded wreckage that had supported me.

'As if from death's door I crawled up and away, gaining strength as I went, until I reached a point from which I could view the nature of the island. Allah! What a paradise it was! Streams of fresh, pure water wimpled down between banks where grew the lordliest trees laden with the rarest fruits. The sight gave me fresh strength. I rose and wandered from stream to stream, drinking the cool water and plucking and eating the delicious fruit. But, O Sindbad the Landsman, though I knew it not, there was a vile snake in this paradise, as I was soon to discover to my cost.

'Coming at length to a stream of some width, I sat down upon a mossy bank with my back against a tree to watch the rippling current purling by. Lulled by this and the songs of the birds, I became drowsy and turned to find a soft bed on the moss, when I caught sight of an object which arrested my attention. There, sitting against the tree next to mine, was an aged man of comely and benevolent aspect.

'I regarded him intently. What a kindly old man he looked, with his flowing silver locks and his ample white beard! The more did I consider him one of nature's innocent children from the fact that his body was clothed from the waist downwards with the green leaves of trees—a raiment neatly threaded together on the fibres of some plant. As I scrutinized his appearance intently for some moments, I felt that here was one of the simplest and kindliest dispositions, who knew not the meaning of wrong. I arose and advanced towards him, but, when I spoke, he shook his head sadly and sighed. Alas! Was he deprived of the power of speech? To make certain, I saluted him, saying, "Allah be with thee!" But he merely bowed his head, making no other reply. All my questions brought never a word: he was, indeed, dumb. But he could make intelligent signs, and I perceived by these that it was his greatest wish to be carried across the stream. Seeing that he was old and infirm as well as dumb, I readily consented. My heart was sorry for him, and I bent down and told him to climb upon my shoulders. This he did with alacrity, and so I carried him over the stream.

'But, when I bent down for him to dismount on the further bank, he showed no manner of inclination to do so. On the contrary, he gripped me with both hands round my throat, and beat me violently in the ribs with his heels. What with the throttling, and the hard blows with his heels, I swooned away; but, notwithstanding, when I regained my senses I found the old fellow still clinging like a leech to my neck. And now he belaboured me so unmercifully that I was forced to rise against my will.

'Once on my feet I determined to shake him off, but he rode me well, and even my efforts to crush him against the trunks of trees were of no avail. I ran hither and thither wildly, employing every trick against him, but all in vain: he kept his seat, and with hand and heel punished me severely. In less than an hour I was broken to the will of this truculent fellow, and he guided me hither and thither among the fruit trees, pulling me up when he would gather fruit and eat, and urging me on again when he so desired.

'In this fashion he stuck to me all that day, and such was his behaviour that I forswore my first opinion of him. He was by no means the gentle being I had thought him. Though he clung so close we were not friends, nor likely to become such. I was his bond-slave, and he ceased not to remind me of it by his utterly vile behaviour. When I dallied he thrashed me unmercifully with his feet; when I thought to brush him off against the overhanging branch of a tree he would duck his head and throttle me with his long bony hands. At night, when I slept exhausted, I woke to find him digging his heels into me in his sleep; indeed, once it seemed that I had thwarted him in a dream, for he thrashed me and treated me abominably. I thought my end had come.

'Thus, for many days and nights was I beridden by this abandoned fellow, forced hither and thither at his will, with never a word from him, though he had many from me. So great was my agony that I turned upon myself, crying, "By the living Allah! Never again will I do a kindness to any; never again will I show mercy!"

'Long I pondered by what subtle trick I might unseat him. I thought of many things, but dared not try one of them, lest it should fail and I be punished unmercifully. But at last Allah took pity on me and threw a strange opportunity in my way.

'It chanced that, one day, while I was being goaded about the island, we came upon a place where pumpkins grew. They were ripe and luscious, and, while the old fellow was eating greedily, I bethought me of a fashion of our own country. I gathered some of the largest, and, having scooped them out, I filled them with the juice squeezed from grapes which I found growing in abundance nearby. Then I sealed them up and set them in the sun. In this way, I obtained in a few days a good quantity of pure wine.

'The old man did not notice my curious behaviour—he was always engaged in eating pumpkins—until one day I drank so much of my newly-made wine that I became exalted, and danced and rollicked about with him among the trees. With fist and heel he sought to sober me, requiring to know the reason for my merriment. At length, I took him to the spot where I had laid my pumpkins in the sun, and then, laughing and dancing again, signed to him that they contained pure wine.

'The idea was new to him, but, when he understood that I had drunk with such pleasant results, he insisted on drinking also. So I unsealed one of the pumpkins and handed it to him, whereupon he drank and smacked his lips. Then he drank again and again and again, with evident satisfaction, until the wine taking effect, and the pumpkin being empty, he broke it over my head and bade me hand him another. This also he emptied and broke in the same manner. Being by this time in a state of vile intoxication, he thrashed me thrice round the open space, and then in among the trees, behaving in the wildest manner possible, rocking and rolling from side to side with laughter.

'Now I had not drunk so much of the wine that I could

not see my chance. I adopted the utmost docility, and, never letting him suspect my purpose, contrived to regain the place where I had laid the pumpkins in the sun. As I had expected, he demanded another, and I gave it him. This time he drank half the wine and emptied the remainder over my face—so vile was this creature of sin. Then I perceived with joy that he was losing control of his limbs. He swayed from side to side, and his head lolled. Slowly, I unwound his legs from my neck, and then, with a vicious twist, I flung him on the ground.

'As I looked upon him lying there, my joy turned to uncontrollable fury. I thought of what I had endured at the hands of this aged villain. Should I allow him to live he would surely treat some other poor shipwrecked traveller in the same abominable fashion. The island would be well rid of such an inhuman monster. Without another thought I slew him then and there. May his accursed spirit be ridden forever by one worse than himself!

'I went forth upon the island like one walking on air. Never was mortal man rid of so heavy a burden as I had just flung from me. Even the very atmosphere of the place seemed light and joyous with relief. The streams rippled more merrily, the birds sang more sweetly, the dreamy trees sighed with content as if at a great and long-desired riddance. They all seemed to feel that this terrible old man no longer oppressed them; his legs were no longer round their necks, his masterful feet and hands no longer gripped them in a vice. Rid—all was rid of an intolerable burden. Having found a shady spot, I sank down on the bank of a stream and wiped my brow, thanking Allah devoutly for this sweet deliverance.

'For long days, thereafter, I sat by the seashore, scanning the ocean for the speck of a sail. But none came in sight, and I was abandoning myself to the thought that Allah had rescued me from one peril only to consign me into the hands of another—that of death by desolation—when one morning I descried a large ship standing in towards the shore. She cast her anchor, and many passengers landed on the island. With a great shout of joy I ran down to greet them. Many voices answered mine, and all plied me with questions respecting my condition. Presently, perceiving that my case was extraordinary, they ceased their questioning while I told them my story. They listened with amazement. Then someone said:

"'In my travels in these seas I have heard many tales of such an old man of whom thou speakest, dwelling alone upon an island, and lying in wait for shipwrecked sailors. I know not how these tales were spread abroad, for it is said that of those he has ridden none has survived. Thou art the only survivor. His name is called the Old Man of the Sea. But now he is no more: Allah be praised for that! And thou bast escaped: Allah be praised for that also!" And all extolled the greatness of Allah.

'I returned with them to the ship, and they clothed me in rich apparel and set food and wine before me; and, when I had refreshed myself, we made merry as the ship set sail.

'We were bound for El-Basrah, and my thoughts flew further—to Baghdad, the Abode of Peace.'

THE COW OF PLENTY

There was a wonderful cow called Surabhi, who belonged to the sage Vasishtha. The cow gave her fortunate owner anything that he wanted: food and drink, clothes and even luxuries. Whenever her owner said the word 'Give', the cow was there to give him the thing he desired. It was not surprising that jealousy and greed were roused in the hearts of those who saw or heard of this wonderful creature.

It so happens that a powerful king, Vishwamitra, was on a hunting expedition which brought him, with many of his followers, to the hermitage of Vasishtha. The holy man greeted the King with great courtesy, then called upon the cow to produce a sumptuous feast for his guests. Immediately, food and drink issued from the cow in an endless stream.

The King was delighted. But he felt envious too. And soon he was asking himself why a hermit in the forest should possess such a splendid creature. It would be more reasonable, he thought, if the cow were in his own hands to provide him with his many needs.

'I'll give you ten thousand cows in exchange for this one,' he told the sage.

When Vasishtha refused to listen to the proposal, the King offered him his entire kingdom.

The sage refused this generous offer, saying that the cow not only supplied him with his own necessities, but also served a similar purpose for the gods and the spirits of the dead.

'Don't forget that I am a king,' said Vishwamitra, 'and when kings can't get what they want, they take it by force.'

'It is not for me to resist,' said the sage. 'I am only a hermit and a scholar. My life is devoted to the study of the sacred books. I cannot set myself against the might of your armed men. Kings do what they like, and take what they want, and never give it a moment's thought.'

The King grew impatient, put a rope round the cow's neck, and began to lead her away.

Surabhi was very unwilling to go. She turned her soft, pathetic eyes towards the sage and refused to move. The King struck her several times with a stick.

At first, the sage said nothing. Then he spoke to the cow: 'My dear and loving Surabhi, I understand your feelings, and I do not wish to lose you. But what can I do? The King is all-powerful. He is taking you away by force and I cannot prevent him.'

When the cow heard these words she broke away from her captor and came running to the sage.

'Do you wish me to go?' she cried. 'Have you lost all affection for me? Do you not care whether the King ill-treats me or not? Have you given me up completely?'

'What can I say?' said the sage. 'A warrior's strength lies in the force at his command. A hermit's strength lies in the spirit of forgiveness he shows. I cannot stop him from taking you, but I certainly do not abandon you or wish you to go.'

'I won't be taken by force,' said the cow. 'If you say you want me with you, that is enough!'

As she spoke, her whole appearance underwent an amazing change. Her eyes flashed fire. Her head and neck grew to an enormous size, and she rushed at the King and his followers. Even more wonderful, great showers of burning coals poured from her tail, and the coals were followed by troops of soldiers. They came not only from her tail, but from her udder and her sides, and from the froth of her mouth. These warriors belonged to many countries and races of men—Greeks, Huns, Scythians, Parthians and Chinese—and they all wore the garments and carried the weapons peculiar to their country.

As they poured forth, they attacked the King and his men with great fury. But they inflicted no injury on them. They were content to give them a good fright. Although they chased Vishwamitra and his men for a distance of seventy-five miles, they did not kill any of them.

By the time the King had recovered his breath, he was already a changed man. He had boasted that kings could do as they liked. But now he realized that kings were really feeble compared with men of wisdom and piety. So he gave up his kingdom and went to live in a forest. He decided that he would persuade the gods to make him one of their priests. And finally, after many years of hardship, prayer and meditation, he achieved his goal and became a true sage.

SHAKUNTALA

In ancient India, when the great God Indra was worshipped, there lived a young king named Dushyanta.

One day, while he was hunting in a great forest, the King became separated from his followers. He wandered on alone through the forest until he found himself in a pleasant grove which led to a hermitage. The little dwelling was the home of an old hermit called Father Kanva. The king had heard many stories about the piety and wisdom of the old man, and decided to honour him with a visit.

To the King's disappointment, however, the hermitage was empty. He turned away and was about to leave the grove when a gentle voice said, 'Wait, my lord,' and a girl stepped out from behind the trees.

In spite of her poor clothes, the girl was so beautiful and dignified that the King's admiration was aroused and he asked her courteously, 'Isn't this the dwelling-place of holy Kanva?'

'Yes, my lord,' she replied. 'But my father is away on a pilgrimage. Will you not rest here a while?'

She brought him water and fruits for his refreshment, and the King was delighted at the hospitality he was shown. It was clear to him that she did not recognize him as the King; so Dushyanta, who liked to mingle unrecognized among his people, pretended to be a huntsman, and asked the girl her name.

'I am called Shakuntala,' she said. 'I am Father Kanva's adopted daughter.'

Encouraged to go on, she told the King that she had been left an orphan when she was very small, and that Kanva had treated her as lovingly as if he had really been her father. Though she was of noble birth, she was very happy living a simple life in the forest.

As Dushyanta listened to her and watched her beautiful face, he felt that he could linger in that enchanting spot forever; but he knew that his followers must be anxiously searching for him, so he took leave of Shakuntala and made his way back to the hunting party.

But he did not leave the forest. Instead he ordered his men to encamp at some distance from the hermitage. The next day, and the following day as well, found him visiting Shakuntala at the hermitage.

Dushyanta and Shakuntala were soon confessing their love for each other; but when the girl learnt that it was the King himself who wished to marry her, she protested that he would surely regret such a hasty decision. Dushyanta, however, soothed her fears, and, dreading lest something might come between them, persuaded her to wed him without delay.

There was no need for a priest to marry the lovers, since, in those days, it was lawful for Kings and warriors to wed their brides by a simple exchange of flowers or garlands. And so Dushyanta and Shakuntala vowed to be true to each other forever.

'Come with me to my palace,' said the King. 'My people shall acknowledge you as their queen.'

'I cannot leave the forest until I have told Father Kanva of our marriage,' said Shakuntala. 'I must wait for him to return. But you must return to your palace to carry out your duties. When you come again, I will be ready to join you.'

The King placed a ring, engraven with the name 'Dushyanta', upon her finger, and promised to return soon.

When he had left, Shakuntala wandered dreamily about the forest, forgetting that someone might visit the hermitage to see Father Kanva. At nightfall when she returned to the grove, she was met by a visitor who was spluttering with rage.

The visitor was an old sage named Durvasas, who was dreaded by all because of his violent temper. It was said that if anyone offended him, he would punish them severely. He was known as a 'master-curser.'

The sage had been waiting at the hermitage a long time, and felt that he had been insulted by Shakuntala. She pleaded for forgiveness, and begged him to stay; but the old man was in a terrible mood. Thrusting the girl aside, he hurried away muttering a curse under his breath.

Shakuntala was troubled not so much by the curse as by the feeling that she had neglected her duties; for in India it is something of a sin if one receives a visitor and allows the guest to depart unhonoured.

Then something happened which worried Shakuntala even more. Whilst she was bathing in the stream near her home, the ring, the King's gift, slipped from her finger and disappeared in the water.

Shakuntala wept bitterly at her loss; but she was not to know what heartbreak it was to bring her in the future, or how closely her bad luck was connected with the angry sage Durvasas.

It was a great relief to her when Father Kanva returned from his pilgrimage. He was not displeased at the news of her marriage to Dushyanta. On the contrary, he was overjoyed.

'My daughter, you are worthy of the King,' he said. 'Gladly will I give you to Dushyanta when he comes to claim you.'

But the days passed, and King Dushyanta did not come.

Shakuntala felt a great weight begin to press against her heart. What could have happened? Was Dushyanta ill, or had he repented of his rash marriage? But no, she could never believe that...

Then Father Kanva, growing uneasy, said: 'My daughter, since the King does not come, you must seek him in his palace. For though it grieves me to part with you, a wife's place is by her husband's side.'

Dushyanta had asked her to wait for him; but she could not refuse to do Father Kanva's bidding. And so, for the first time in her life, she left her forest home and journeyed to the unknown world beyond.

After several days she reached the royal city, and, learning that the King was in his palace, she asked permission to see him, saying that she had brought a message from Father Kanva.

When she found herself at the foot of the King's throne, she looked up so that he could see her face, and said, 'Do not be angry with me, my lord, but since you did not keep your promise to claim me soon, I have been forced to seek you here.'

'My promise to claim you?' King Dushyanta looked bewildered. 'What do you mean?'

Shakuntala looked at him with fear in her eyes.

'You are mocking me, my lord,' she said. 'Have you forgotten our marriage in the forest, and how you said you would cherish me forever? Do not look so strangely at me, I beg you, but acknowledge me as your bride!'

'My bride!' exclaimed the King. 'What fantasy is this? I have never seen you before!'

Shakuntala was astounded. What has happened to him? she wondered. I have always dreaded that he would repent of our hasty marriage. But surely he would not deny me? And she stretched out her arms to him and cried, 'How can you say such words?

They are not worthy of a King. What have I done that you should treat me so cruelly?'

'I have never seen you before,' said the King firmly. 'You must be either mad or wicked to come to me with such a tale.'

Shakuntala stood looking at him with growing despair in her heart. Then, realizing from the King's hard countenance the hopelessness of her situation, she fled from the palace, weeping bitterly.

Now, although King Dushyanta appeared to have become callous and cruel in such a short space of time, in reality he had only spoken what he believed to be the truth. He did not remember Shakuntala at all, and for a very good reason. When the old sage Durvasas had muttered his curse, he had decreed, first of all, that she should lose the King's ring, and then, that until Dushayanta saw the ring again, he would be unable to remember Shakuntala, even though she stood before him.

Not even the God Indra could alter a curse once it had been pronounced by the old sage, and since Dushyanta's ring had been swept away by the stream in the forest, there was little hope that he would ever remember his bride.

Several years passed, and then one day a fisherman was brought before the King to relate a curious story.

The fisherman had caught a fine carp in the river, and when he had cut the fish open, a gold ring engraven with the name 'Dushyanta' was found within the body of the carp.

The King examined the ring with interest. 'It does look like mine,' he said, 'yet I don't remember losing it.'

He rewarded the fisherman for his honesty, and after examining the ring again, he placed it upon his finger.

'How strange!' he said. 'A cloud seems to be lifting from my mind. Yes, I remember now—this is the ring I gave to my bride, Shakuntala, in the forest. Ah, but what have I done! It was Shakuntala who came to me that day, and I sent her from me with cruel words.'

Dushyanta hastened to the forest, but the hermitage was deserted. Father Kanva was long since dead. The King had the land searched, but it was as though Shakuntala had vanished from the earth. He fell into a deep melancholy from which no one could rouse him.

But although the God Indra had not been able to avert the curse of Durvasas, he had not been indifferent to the suffering that had been caused. And now that the ring had been recovered, he was determined to help the unhappy King.

One day, Dushyanta was walking in his garden when he saw a strange object in the sky. It looked like a great shining bird.

As it came nearer, the bird proved to be a chariot drawn by prancing horses, whose reins were held by a celestial-looking being.

The chariot alighted on the earth not far from the King, and the charioteer called: 'Dushyanta! Do you not know me? I am Matali, the charioteer of great Indra. Come with me, for Indra has need of you.'

Dushyanta was awestruck; but he stepped into the chariot and was whirled upwards so swiftly that soon his kingdom lay like a speck beneath him. The chariot soared still higher, and the horses trod the air as if it were solid ground beneath their feet. Then suddenly the chariot stopped in the midst of the clouds, and Matali told Dushyanta to descend.

The King obeyed, and gradually, as the mist cleared and the clouds melted away, he saw that he was alone in a beautiful garden. He felt that surely he was near great Indra's dwelling.

There was a rustling in the bushes, and Dushyanta waited breathlessly. Perhaps the God was about to reveal himself.

It was not a heavenly being who appeared, however, but a

little boy who was carrying a lion cub. The cub struggled fiercely in his arms, but the boy held on to it without fear.

'Come here, boy,' called the King. 'Tell me your name.'

'I do not know it,' said the boy.

'That is strange,' said Dushyanta. He felt irresistibly drawn towards the boy, and held out his hand to him, but the boy drew back.

'No one shall touch me,' he said, and then called out: 'Mother, come quickly!'

'I am coming, son,' said a gentle voice.

The King stepped back, trembling violently, for there before him stood Shakuntala, looking pale and sad but more beautiful than ever.

When she saw the King she drew herself up proudly, but Dushyanta fell at her feet, crying: 'Shakuntala, do not turn from me. Listen, I beg of you!' And he told her of how he had forgotten her until the recovery of the ring, and of how he had since sought her everywhere.

Shakuntala's face lit up with joy and she cried, 'Oh, Dushyanta, now I understand. It must have been the punishment of Durvasas.' And she told him about the curse of the angry sage, how she had lost her ring in the stream, and how she had suffered all these years at the thought of her husband's denial of her.

'But where have you been all the time?' asked Dushyanta. 'What is the place?'

'This is a sacred mountain near the dwelling-place of great Indra. When you denied me in your palace, I felt that I should die of grief. But a wonderful thing happened to me. As I lay weeping on the ground, Indra send his chariot to earth, and I was brought here by heavenly beings who have watched over us all this time.'

'Mother,' cried the boy, who had been watching from a little distance. 'Who is this man?'

'Your father, my child,' said Shakuntala. 'Embrace your son, Dushyanta. He was a gift from the gods to comfort me in my loneliness.'

And as Dushyanta knelt down to embrace his son, Matali again appeared in his chariot.

'Are you happy, Dushyanta?' he asked, 'Now it is Indra's wish that you return with me to earth. Cherish your son, happy mortals, for he shall become the founder of a race of heroes.'

The chariot took them back to earth, and from that time Dushyanta and Shakuntala lived in great happiness, while their son, whom they named Bharata, grew up to found a noble race, as Matali had foretold.

THE CRANE AND THE CRAB

Every summer the water in the village pond fell very low, and one could see the fish swimming about near the bottom. A crane caught sight of them and said to himself, 'I must find a way to get hold of those fish.' And he sat down in deep thought by the side of the pond.

When the fish caught sight of the crane, they said, 'Of what are you thinking, my lord, as you sit there?'

'I am thinking about you,' said the crane. 'The water in this pool being very low, the heat so great, and food so very scarce, I was wondering what in the world you fishes were going to do!'

'And what do you suggest we do, sir?'

'Well, if you agree, I will take you up one by one in my beak, and carry you off to a fine large pool covered with five different kinds of lotus-flowers, and there I will put you down.'

'But, good sir,' they said, 'no crane ever took the slightest thought for the welfare of a fish ever since the world began. Your desire is to eat us, one by one.'

'No, I will not eat you while you trust me,' said the crane. 'If you don't take my word that there is such a pool, send one of your number to go with me and see for himself.'

Believing this to be a fair proposal, the fish presented the crane with a great big fish (blind in one eye), who they thought would be a match for the crane whether on land or water. The crane carried the fish off and dropped him in the pool, and after allowing him to take a good look at it, brought him back to his old pond. Then he told all the other fish about the charms of the new pool.

The fish became eager to go there, and said to the crane, 'We shall be grateful, my lord, if you would kindly take us across.'

Well, to begin with, the crane took the big one-eyed fish again and carried him off to the new pool; but instead of dropping the fish in the water, the crane alighted in a tree which grew at the edge of the pool. Dashing the fish down in a fork of the tree, the crane pecked it to death. He then picked it clean and let the bones fall at the foot of the tree.

When the crane returned to the pond, he said, 'I've thrown him in. Who's next?'

And so he took the fish one by one, and ate them all. But there was still a crab remaining in the muddy waters of the pond. And the crane wanted to eat him too.

'Mister crab,' he said, 'I've carried all those fine fish away and dropped them into a beautiful large pool. Come along, I'll take you there too.'

'And how will you carry me across?' asked the crab.

'In my beak, of course.'

'Ah, but you might drop me like that.' And to himself he said: 'He hasn't put the fish in the pool, that's certain. But if he would really put me in, it would be wonderful. I could do with a change. And, if he *doesn't*—well, I think I know how to deal with him!' And he spoke to the crane: 'You won't be able to hold me tight enough, friend crane. But we crabs have a very firm grip. If I might take hold of your neck with my claws, I could hold on tight and go along with you.'

The crane agreed, and the crab took hold of the bird's neck with his pincers, and said, 'Let's go.' The crane flew him across and showed him the pool, and then started off for the tree.

'You're going the wrong way, friend,' said the crab.

'Don't call me friend,' said the crane. 'I suppose you thought me your slave to lift you up and carry you about! Well, just take a look at that heap of bones at the foot of the tree. As I ate up all those fish, so I will eat you too.'

'It was because of their own foolishness that the fish were eaten,' said the crab. 'I won't be giving you the same opportunity. If we die, we will die together.' And he tightened his grip on the crane's long neck.

With his mouth open and the tears streaming from his eyes, the crane gasped, 'Lord, indeed I will not eat you! Spare my life!'

'Well then, just step down to the pool and put me in,' said the crab.

The crane turned back to the pool, and placed the crab in the mud at the water's edge.

'Thank you, friend,' said the crab, and nipped off the crane's head as neatly as if he were cutting a lotus-stalk with a knife.

TORIA AND THE DAUGHTER OF THE SUN

Once upon a time there was a young shepherd of the Santal tribe named Toria, who grazed his sheep and goats on the bank of a river. Now it happened that the daughters of the Sun would descend from heaven every day by means of a spider's web, to bathe in the river. Finding Toria there, they invited him to bathe with them. After they had bathed and anointed themselves with oils and perfumes, they returned to their heavenly abode, while Toria went to look after his flock.

Having become friendly with the daughters of the Sun, Toria gradually fell in love with one of them. But he was at a loss to know how to obtain such a divine creature. One day, when they met him and said, 'Come along, Toria, and bathe with us,' he suddenly thought of a plan.

While they were bathing, he said, 'Let us see who can stay under water the longest.' At a given signal they all dived, but very soon Toria raised his head above water and, making sure that no one was looking, hurried out of the water, picked up the robe of the girl he loved, and was in the act of carrying it away when the others raised their heads above the water.

The girl ran after him, begging him to return her garment, but Toria did not stop till he had reached his home. When she arrived, he gave her the robe without a word. Seeing such a beautiful and noble creature before him, for very bashfulness he could not open his mouth to ask her to marry him; so he simply said, 'You can go now.'

But she replied, 'No, I will not return. My sisters by this time will have gone home. I will stay with you, and be your wife.'

All the time this was going on, a parrot, whom Toria had taught to speak, kept on flying about the heavens, calling out to the Sun: 'Oh, great Father, do not look downwards!' As a result, the Sun did not see what was happening on earth to his daughter.

This girl was very different from the women of the country she was half human, half divine—so that when a beggar came to the house and saw her, his eyes were dazzled just as if he had stared at the Sun.

It happened that this same beggar in the course of his wanderings came to the King's palace, and having seen the queen, who was thought by all to be the most beautiful of women, he told the King: 'The shepherd Toria's wife is far more beautiful than your queen. If you were to see her, you would be enchanted.'

'How can I see her?' asked the King eagerly.

The beggar answered, 'Put on your old clothes and travel in disguise.'

The King did so, and having arrived at the shepherd's house, asked for alms. Toria's wife came out of the house and gave him food and water, but he was so astonished at seeing her great beauty that he was unable to eat or drink. His only thought was, 'How can I manage to make her my queen?

When he got home he thought over many plans and at length decided upon one. He said, 'I will order Toria to dig a large tank with his own hands, and fill it with water, and if he does not perform the task, I will kill him and seize his wife.' He then summoned Toria to the palace, commanded him to dig the tank and threatened him with death if he failed to fill the tank with water the same night.

Toria returned home slowly and sorrowfully.

'What makes you so sad today?' asked his wife.

He replied, 'The King has ordered me to dig a large tank, to fill it with water, and also to make trees grow beside it, all in the course of one night.'

'Don't let it worry you,' said his wife. 'Take your spade and mix a little water with the sand, where the tank is to be, and it will form there by itself.'

Toria did as he was told, and the King was astonished to find the tank completed in time. He had no excuse for killing Toria.

Later, the King planted a great plant with mustard seed. When it was ready for reaping, he commanded Toria to reap and gather the produce into one large heap on a certain day; failing which, he would certainly be put to death.

Toria, hearing this, was again very sad. When he told his wife about it, she said, 'Do not worry, it will be done.' So the daughter of the Sun summoned her children, the doves. They came in large numbers, and in the space of an hour carried the produce away to the King's threshing-floor. Again, Toria was saved through the wisdom of his wife. However, the King determined not to be outdone, so he arranged a great hunt. On the day of the hunt he assembled his retainers, and a large number of beaters and provision-carriers, and set out for the jungle. Toria was employed to carry eggs and water. But the objective of the hunt was not to kill a tiger, it was to kill Toria, so that the King might seize the daughter of the Sun and make her his wife.

Arriving at a cave, they said that a hare had taken refuge in it. They forced Toria into the cave. Then, rolling large stones against the entrance, they completely blocked it. They gathered large quantities of brushwood at the mouth of the cave, and set fire to it to smother Toria. Having done this, they returned home, boasting that they had finally disposed of the shepherd. But Toria broke the eggs, and all the ashes were scattered. Then he poured the water that he had with him on the remaining embers, and the fire was extinguished. Toria managed to crawl out of the cave. And there, to his great astonishment, he saw that all the white ashes of the fire were becoming cows, whilst the half-burnt wood was turning into buffaloes.

Toria herded the cows and buffaloes together, and drove them home.

When the King saw the herd, he became very envious, and asked Toria where he had found such fine cows and buffaloes. Toria said, 'From that cave into which you pushed me. I did not bring many with me, being on my own. But if you and all your retainers go, you will be able to get as many as you want. But to catch them it will be necessary to close the door of the cave, and light a fire in front, as you did for me.'

'Very well,' said the King. 'My people and I will enter the cave, and, as you have sufficient cows and buffaloes, kindly do not go into the cave with us, but kindle the fire outside.'

The King and his people then entered the cave. Toria blocked up the doorway, and then lit a large fire at the entrance. Before long, all that were in the cave were suffocated.

Some days later the daughter of the Sun said, 'I want to visit my father's house.'

Toria said, 'Very well, I will also go with you.'

'No, it is foolish of you to think of such a thing,' she said. 'You will not be able to get there.'

'If you are able to go, surely I can.' And he insisted on accompanying her.

After travelling a great distance, Toria became so faint from the heat of the sun that he could go no further. His wife said,

'Did I not warn you? As for quenching your thirst, there is no water to be found here. But sit down and rest, I will see if I can find some for you.'

While she was away, driven by his great thirst, Toria sucked a raw egg that he had brought with him. No sooner had he done this than he changed into a fowl. When his wife returned with water, she could not find him anywhere; but, sitting where she had left him, was a solitary fowl. Taking the bird in her arms, she continued her journey.

When she reached her father's house, her sisters asked her, 'Where is Toria, your husband?' She replied, 'I don't know. I left him on the road while I went to fetch water. When I returned, he had disappeared. Perhaps he will turn up later.'

Her sisters, seeing the fowl, thought that it would make a good meal. And so, while Toria's wife was resting, they killed and ate the fowl. Later, when they again enquired of her as to the whereabouts of her husband, she looked thoughtful.

'I can't be sure,' she said. 'But I think you have eaten him.'

THE WICKED GURU

A certain king of the South had a beautiful daughter. When she had reached a marriageable age, the King spoke to his Guru (spiritual teacher) and said: 'Tell me, O Guru, by the stars the auspicious day for my daughter's marriage.'

But the Guru had become enamoured of the girl's beauty, and he answered with guile, 'It will be wrong to celebrate your daughter's marriage at this time. It will bring evil on both of you. Instead, adorn her with thirty-six ornaments and clothe her in the finest of her garments, cover her with flowers and sprinkle her with perfumes, and then set her in a spacious box afloat on the waters of the ocean.'

It was the time of Dwapara Yuga—the third age of the world—and the Guru had to be obeyed. So they did as he said, to the great sorrow of the King and all his subjects. The King asked the Guru to stay and comfort them, but he said he had to return at once to his sacred seat, and left for his own home some three days distant.

As soon as he reached his house, the Guru stocked it with gold and pearl and silver and coral and the finest of fabrics that women delight in, and called his three hundred and sixty disciples and said: 'My children, go and search the ocean, and whoever finds floating on it a large box, bring it here, and do not come to me again until I summon you.'

They all scattered to do as they had been told.

Meanwhile, the King of a neighbouring country had gone hunting on the sea-shore, where he had wounded a bear in the leg. The wounded bear limped about and gave vent to short savage grunts. As the King looked out to sea, he saw a box floating on the crests of the waves. He was quite a young man, and, being an expert swimmer, he soon brought the box ashore. Great was his surprise and joy to find that it contained a beautiful girl adorned as a bride.

He put the lame bear into the box and set it afloat once again. Then he hurried home with his prize. The girl was only too glad to marry her deliverer, and a great wedding took place.

All this time the Guru's disciples were searching for the box, and when one of them found it floating near the shore he duly brought it to the Guru, and then disappeared as he had been told. The Guru was delighted. He prepared sweets, fruits, flowers and scents. He closed all the doors of his chamber. He could hardly contain himself as he opened the box.

As soon as the box was open, out jumped the bear, savage and hungry and at war with all human beings because of the treatment he had received. He seized the Guru in a bear-hug and then tore out his throat.

Feeling his life ebbing, the Guru dipped his finger in his own blood and wrote this shloka:

Man's desires are not fulfilled.
The God's desires prevail.
The king's daughter is in the king's palace.
The bear has eaten the priest.

When the Guru failed to send for his disciples, they went together to his house, where, on breaking open his chamber-door, they found his body. The Guru's murder appeared to be a mystery, until the King, who had been sent for, found the verses on the wall and had them translated by his scholars. One scholar proved that the bear could have escaped by means of a large drain that was found in the building.

Now it happened that this King was related to the neighbouring King who had found and married the princess in the box, and went to visit him.

'How remarkably like my daughter,' he remarked, on seeing his hostess.

'Yes, the same daughter who was set afloat in a box,' said the Queen. But they were overjoyed to see each other again; and the King was especially pleased, because he had all along hoped that his daughter would marry the King-next-door.

THE TULIP PIXIES

Down in the West, somewhere by the borders of the Tavy, there once lived a kind old woman. Her cottage was was near a pixie field, where green rings stood in the grass. Now some folk say those fairy rings are caused by the elves catching colts. They catch them and ride them round and round by night, such folk do say. But this old woman had other ideas about her fairy rings.

Around her tidy cottage was a pretty garden, full of sweet-smelling flowers. Lavender and holly hocks grew there, lilies and rosemary and the sweet briar tree, blue-buttons and gilly-flowers, forget-me-nots and rue. But best of all was a big bed of tulips which she tended with special care. Everyone stopped to peep over her gate when the time of tulips came.

How the pixies loved this spot. They liked the kind old woman, and they liked her garden too.

One starry night, as she lay asleep, with the lilac flowers showing white under her window, she was awakened by a strange sound. At first, she thought an owl in the elm tree had wakened her, but gradually she realized that it was a sweeter sound than the crack of the churn owl.

'It does sound for all the world like a lullaby,' she thought and lay listening for a while.

Then she got out of bed and peered from the window. There below her in the moonlight all the tulips in their shining colours were waving their heads in tune with the sweet music. It seemed as though they themselves were singing too.

Now when this happened the next night, and the next, the old woman began to understand what had happened. The pixie folk had brought their babies to the tulip bed, and laid each one within a separate flower.

'They be lullin' their babies to sleep, I do declare,' said the old woman, delighted. 'Ssh! I see them now. The pixie babies are fast asleep, and there go the pixie folk themselves to dance in the meadow grass.'

She was right. It was not the catching of colts that made those rings on the green grass, but the dancing of the little folk to their own pipers' tune. But as the first clawn light broke pale in the cast back came the pixies to claim their babies from the tulip cradles, where they lay asleep. And, all invisible now, they vanished clean away.

She noticed that the tulips did not fade so quickly as the other flowers in the garden. Indeed, it seemed as though they would never wither. And one day, as she bent to have a look at them, the old woman noticed that the pixies had made them even lovelier by breathing over them. Now they smelled as fragrant as lilies or roses do.

'No one, shall pick a single tulip, not even myself,' she said. They shall be kept altogether for the pixies' own delight.'

And so it was as year succeeded year.

But no one lives forever, and at last the old woman died. It was a sad day for the garden, and the tulips hung their heads. Well they might, for presently the garden passed into other hands. The new tenant cared nothing for pixie lore. He only cared for the garden at all because of its trees of fruit. Gooseberries and raspberries and greengage-plums made very tasty pies!

'You shouldn't be gatherin' the gooseberries out of season,' a neighbour warned him, 'Tis proper unlucky. The pixies can't abide bein' robbed of their own.'

'Pixies? Pah!' said the man.

'Surely ye aint a-digging up they tulips?' said another. 'Twas the old woman's special delight that bed o' flowers. What be yu puttin' in?'

'I be settin' a bed of parsley, if you must know,' said the man. 'Parsley? Dear soul alive! Don't you know 'tis mortal unlucky to set a parsley bed. Last man as ever I heard of was bedridden ever after.'

'Stuff and nonsense!' snapped the new tenant disbelievingly.

So the enchanted flowers were rooted up, and parsley set instead. But so offended were the pixies that they caused it to wither away. Not only would nothing grow in the gay tulip bed, but the whole garden was soon a waste.

Yet though the lullabies were heard no more from the tulip bed, singing still came from the little folk who dwelt in the neighbourhood. But this time the singing came from the old woman's grave. Sad and sorrowful was the song the pixies sang, and every night before the moon was full they sang it.

No one looked after the old woman's grave, yet never a weed was seen. As she had tended their tulip bed, so now they tended her grave. And though no one was ever seen to plant a flower, somehow her favourites sprang up in the night—rosemary and gilly-flowers, lavender and forget-me-nots.

I cannot tell how the truth may be.
I say the tale as 'twas said to me.

THE CLICKING TOAD

Once upon a time—and a very good time it was—when pigs were swine and dogs ate lime, and monkeys chewed tobacco, when houses were thatched with pancakes, streets paved with plum puddings, and roasted pigs ran up and down the streets with knives and forks on their backs, crying, 'Come and eat me!' that was a good time for travellers.

And this particular traveller, who had come to Darlaston on business, betook himself for a walk in the fields beyond the town while he was waiting for his return coach. It was an evening in late summer, still but close. The harvest had begun and the oats were already stooked; and the partridges were feeding in the bond stubble. The thrushes and blackbirds had finished singing, and only the woodpigeons, hidden in the tops of the elms, tried over their unfinished cooings.

The pastures tempted the traveller, for most of his days were spent in towns. He climbed stiles, wandered here and there, meeting nobody but an old gaffer whom he greeted with, 'We've had a lot of rain, I see.'

'I know'd we should,' said the old fellow. 'Saturday moon and Sunday full, allus brings rain.'

The traveller passed on, smelling the late honeysuckle and prying for berries. And he heated himself so much that he grew impatient with his heavy clothes. He took off his waistcoat and threw it over his arm and, as he walked from hedge to hedge and reached now to this bough and now to that, he did not notice his watch slip from his waistcoat pocket and waistcoat pocket and fall without a sound between two tussocks. Not even when he was in the coach, an hour later, and on his way home, did he realize he had lost his watch. While the coach wheels spun merrily over the road, it lay where it had fallen, ticking away to the grasshoppers and the ants and the ladybirds that lived in the grasses around it.

It was a fine watch, with a full white face, slender pointers, and a loud clear tick; and as the evening came on and the day grew cool, and the last birds silenced themselves, its ticking seemed to grow louder and louder, as if the watch were alive and were asking to be found and taken from its prison between the tussocks. When the first stars began to show themselves, its white face seemed to grow luminous: from a distance it shone like a mushroom or a rare flower that opened only at night.

No one, however, came that way till night. Then, when the Darlaston bells were ringing curfew and there was no light in the sky except a faint green glimmer in the west, two men came by to look at some snares that they had set. They came guiltily and furtively, for they were poaching; after all, their day was the noon of night. Their ears were open for any strange sound and no sooner had they come within earshot of the watch than they stopped and listened.

'Hark, Bill,' said the first poacher, 'there's something strange here. Hold still and listen.'

''Tis a grasshopper,' replied Bill.

'A grasshopper? I never yet heard the grasshopper that chirped as long as this. Listen to him. He never stops.'

''Tis some thing else then. 'Tis a bird, maybe.'

'If 'its, 'tis a bewitched bird then,' said Tom, and at that moment a breath of wind carried the ticking towards them and made the sound louder than ever.

'Let's track him down,' replied Bill, and cautiously they quartered the ground till they came to the watch.

'There he is. I can see him shining. He has one big eye. Can you see him?'

'That I can, and I don't like the look on him.'

'No more do I. Look, he's ready to spring. A pound to a penny, 'tis something wicked. Come on, let's be off, or he'll be at our throats and sucking our blood afore we know where we are.'

His friend needed no encouragement. Both took to their heels and did not stop running till they were well clear of the one-eyed monster that lurked among the tussocks and ticked so mysteriously.

Once home, they told the story of the strange noise that had alarmed them and by the next morning all Darlaston had heard of the strange creature that lay in the fields, and all Darlaston was curious to peep at it. However, though many peeped, it was a sad truth that not one man, not one woman could tell what it was, for there was no one in Darlaston that had ever before in his life seen a watch. In the end, it was agreed that the solution to the problem should be left to a wise old man who had lived all his life in those parts. To Daddy—for so they called him—they sent a deputation; and word soon went round that Daddy was going forth to make a pronouncement on the riddle.

Daddy was a very old man. His face was shrunk like a long-kept apple and covered with small wrinkles that ran together like cracks in a crock. His eyes were light blue and watery, and he kept his mouth open as if it was too much of an effort for him to hold up his jaw. He was too infirm to walk so they put him in an old wheelbarrow and wheeled him off to the field.

When he came near, the circle round the watch opened, let him in, and then closed again. As the wheelbarrow was halted a silence came over the crowd.

'Take I right up to this object,' said Daddy.

'Why, you be right up to it now,' called the bystanders.

'Then wheel I round the object,' said the old man, and his wheeler took him up and with great gravity wheeled him round.

'Wheel I round again,' said the old man, and it seemed as if he were enjoying being trundled around so. They made a second circuit. 'Now wheel I round a third time.'

The third circuit was completed, the barrow legs were set down and a great silence fell on the crowd. Then, struggling to his feet, the old man lifted up his arms and cried out in a foreboding voice, 'Tis un clicking toad! 'Tis un clicking toad! Lads, arm yourselves with sticks and stones, for the end of the world be coming upon Darlaston!'

When they heard this direful utterance, sticks and stones were the last things that the folks of Darlaston thought of Instead, with yells and shrieks they turned and ran home as fast as they could. To Daddy, trundled along more quickly than ever he had been wheeled before, it seemed as if his prophecy was coming true more quickly than he himself had realized. Man, woman and child, all fled to their homes and barred, bolted and shuttered every door and window. All that day, and all the next day the streets and fields were empty. All Darlaston was indoors waiting for Judgement Day to come.

Of course, Judgement Day did not come. While the people of Darlaston read away at their Bibles, and gabbled at their prayers, all that happened outside was that a traveller got down from the mail coach just outside the town, crossed the field, picked up the watch he had lost, thanked his good fortune, and went away.

Be bow bend it,
My tale's ended.
If you don't like it,
You may mend it.

THE GREEN LADIES OF ONE TREE HILL

Few will need to be told that the Christmas season consists of twelve days besides Christmas Day, which are commonly spoken of in Shropshire as Christmastide. Preparation for Christmas includes a general house-cleaning: everything is scrubbed to the utmost pitch of cleanliness. The pewter and brazen vessels have to be made so bright that the maids can see to put their caps on in them—otherwise the fairies will pinch them. But if all is perfect, the worker will find a coin in her shoe.

Then the clean cheerful family kitchen must be adorned with holly and ivy. Sprigs of bright-berried holly, alternating with darker ivy, are stuck in the small leaded panes of the window casements, among the willow-pattern plates and dishes on the dark oak dresser.

Christmas fare would consist of new beer, and honey, primrose, elderberry and dandelion wines, with roast and boiled beef, hams, hares, geese and fowls, mince and apple pies, junkets, cinnamon cakes, cider cakes and Christmas cakes. Supper fare consists of meat, pig's puddings, pork pies or mince pies, or else of toasted cheese eaten with beer and toast.

And then there were the stories. Here is one from Baslow in Derbyshire.

There were once three tall trees on a hill and on moonlit nights singing could be heard and three Green Ladies danced there. No one dared go near except the farmer and he only climbed the hill once a year on Midsummer Eve to lay a posy of late primroses on the root of each tree. The leaves rustled and the sun shone out, and he made quite sure he was safe indoors before sunset. It was a rich farm and he often said to his three sons, 'My father always said our luck lies up there; when I'm dead don't forget to do as I did, and my father before me, and all our forbears through the years.'

And they listened, but did not take much heed, except the youngest.

When the old man died the big farm was divided into three. The eldest brother took a huge slice, and the next brother took another, and that left the youngest with a strip of poor rough ground at the foot of the hill, but he didn't say much but set to work about it and sang as he worked and was indoors before sunset.

One day, his brothers came to see him. Their big farms were not doing very well and when they saw his rich little barley fields and the few loaded fruit trees, and his roots and herbs growing so green and smelling so sweet, and his three cows giving rich milk, they were angry and jealous.

Who helps you in your work?' they asked. 'They say down in the village there's singing and dancing at night. A hard-working farmer should be abed.'

But the youngest did not answer.

'Did we see you up the hill by the trees as we came? What were you about?'

'I was doing as Father told us years ago. 'Tis Midsummer Eve,' he said quietly enough then.

But they were too angry even to laugh at him.

'The hill is mine,' cried the eldest. 'Don't let me see you up there again. As for the trees, I need timber for my new great barn, so I'm cutting one down. And you two can help me.'

But the second brother found he had to go to market, and the youngest did not answer. The next day, Midsummer Day, the eldest came with carts and men and axes, and called to his youngest brother, who was busy in the herb garden; but he only said, 'Remember what day it is.'

But the eldest and his team went on up the hill to the three trees. When he laid his axe to the first tree it screamed like a woman, the horses ran away and the men after them, but the eldest went on hacking. The wind howled and the two other trees lashed their branches in anger. Then the murdered tree fell down, down on top of him and killed him. By and by his servants came and took the dead man and the dead tree away and then there were only two Green Ladies on moonlit nights.

The second brother came back from market and took both the farms for himself, and the youngest he still worked his little strip of land and took primroses up the hill on Midsummer Eve. But the big farms didn't prosper at all and one Midsummer Eve the second brother saw the youngest brother up by the two trees. He was afraid to go up there, so he yelled.

'Come off my land and take your cows away, breaking my hedges down. I'll build a stout timber fence round my hill and I'll cut down one of the trees to make it with.'

That night there was no dancing together, there was no music but the crying of many leaves, and the youngest brother was very sad. The next morning, the second brother came with an axe and the two trees shuddered; but he only made sure there was no wind to drop the tree his way. The tree screamed like a woman as it fell and the youngest brother watching from the lane below with his cows saw the last tree lift a great branch and bring it down on his brother's head and kill him.

People came and took the second dead tree and man away, and the youngest brother now had all three farms. But he still lived in his little farm near the hill and the lonely Green Lady. And sometimes she would dance alone to a sad little tune on moonlit nights, and he always left a bunch of late primroses at the roots of the one tree every Midsummer Eve and his farms prospered from that day.

There are many people nowadays who won't climb One Tree Hill, especially on Midsummer Eve, and one or two very old people remember being told when they were little children that it must never be fenced because it belonged to a Green Lady.